My Mother's Apprentice

TULSA

ISBN: 978-1-957262-07-9
My Mother's Apprentice

Copyright © 2022 by Gyasi Burks-Abbott
All rights reserved.

For permission requests, write to the publisher at the address below.

Yorkshire Publishing
1425 E 41st Pl
Tulsa, OK 74105
www.YorkshirePublishing.com
918.394.2665

Published in the USA

My Mother's Apprentice

An Autistic's Rites of Passage

Gyasi Burks-Abbott

Dedication

In loving memory of my mother,
Dr. Ruth Elizabeth Burks (1949-2017).

To any parent who worries about the fate of a disabled child.

Contents

Forward

My mom and I had a plan. We would write a book together. It all began with a portrait my mom did of me. Not a portrait done with paint capturing light and shadow but one written with words conveying point-of-view and perspective. My mother was taking a course at the Harvard Graduate School of Education in a social scientific method called Portraiture, in which an investigator attempts to capture the essence of a subject based on observation and interviewing.

The subject my mom chose was me, or more specifically, my autism and what it meant to me. Of course, having been there from the beginning, my mom probably knew more about my autism than I did, but she wanted to see it from my vantage point. As it happens, I had been hoping to share my perspective with the world for years but was having a remarkably difficult time doing so. Getting my thoughts into book form was proving more difficult than either my mom or I could ever have imagined. At the time I sat for my mom's portrait, writing my memoirs was a half-decade old project not completely abandoned but lingering uncomfortably on the back burner. My plan B of pursuing a career in librarianship was also in limbo; I was on leave from my job as a library assistant for the Harvard College Library.

My mom's final paper for the class had the downstream effect of inspiring me to return to my memoirs. It also coincided with a shift in my mom's scholarly interests; a college professor with a Ph.D. in English and a specialization in African American literature and film, my mother, wanted to change her focus and pursue the burgeoning field of Disability Studies. The change wasn't that drastic; it was more of an expansion. In addition to analyzing the representation of African Americans in the media, my mom was now interested in how the disabled were perceived and received in society. In profiling me, my mom wanted to demonstrate the confluence of my intersecting identities (autism and blackness) while also highlighting the contradictions between how I saw myself and how the outside world viewed me.

A version of my mom's portrait entitled "A Brief Portrait of an Autistic as a Young Man" appeared in an anthology called <u>Illness in the Academy: A Collection of Pathographies by Academics.</u> Like the other contributors to <u>Illness in the Academy</u>, my mom merged her professional life as a scholar with her personal experience with disability. As the title implies, every writer was an academic who either had or was close to someone who had a mental or physical medical condition.

As part of a conference called "Autism and Representation," my mother organized a panel of autistic adults that gave me an opportunity to make my own contribution to Disability Studies. The brainchild of another English professor with an autistic son, "Autism and Representation," examined the image of autism in science and popular culture. I presented a paper critiquing the much-talked-about novel <u>The Curious Incident of the Dog in the Night-time,</u> which is told from the point of view of an autistic narrator. Among other things, I addressed the paradox inherent in the non-autistic author's claim that his autistic protagonist could never have written his own book because of an inability to put himself in the reader's shoes. Indeed, a voice was being granted to an autistic perspective while also being denied to actual autistics. My paper would later be published in an anthology called <u>Autism and Representation</u>.

Though most of the conference participants were not autistic, many had a connection to autism either through a child or a sibling. Incidentally, my two fellow panelists were both autistic, and each had an autistic child. So, like with the anthology <u>Illness in the Academy</u>, there was a synergy between the personal and the professional, which produced a plethora of perspectives; the representation of autism in film, literature, and scientific discourse as seen through the eyes of humanists, scientists, parents, and people with autism.

My mom and I also created a PowerPoint presentation addressing the autism epidemic. While the reasons for the increase in autism prevalence were open for debate, there was little doubt that the precipitous rise in the number of autism cases would have a huge impact on society, particularly as these newly diagnosed children grew into adulthood. Our presentation outlined the projected economic cost of autism before telling my story from two complementary perspectives: my mom's and mine.

The presentation, which my mom and I first presented at a Harvard Graduate School of Education conference, was a big hit, and we took it on the road. We delivered different versions of our joint talk in a variety of venues both domestically and internationally. And one of the things that was most appreciated across all audiences was the opportunity to hear from both mom and me. So, my mom and I planned to continue our collaboration in book form in what would be an extended portrait of me. My mother hoped that our project would shed new light on autism while also helping to secure my future. As my mom explained in one of our joint presentations:

> I cherish the sometimes joyous, sometimes tortuous moments I shared with Gyasi providing "Mommy therapy," wearing a head scarf to way-

lay his affectionate, excruciatingly painful vise-like grip on my hair, or teaching him not to walk like a duck or talk like a robot. And I consider myself lucky that, bereft of precedent, I could change his prognosis from a mentally retarded individual unable to graduate from sixth grade to a man whose academic achievements pale in light of his generosity of spirit. At the same time, I know his strengths as well as his weaknesses, so even though Gyasi may currently present on the higher end of the autism spectrum, like every parent of a developmentally disabled adult, I, too, agonize over what's going to happen to him when I "age out" and no one's there to take my place.

Indeed, my mom's fear about what would happen to me after she was gone became far less abstract when she was diagnosed with lung cancer. Also, the plans for our collaboration completely changed, as did our roles. My mom was now the subject, and the condition to be considered, comprehended, and ultimately conquered was cancer.

And my mother and I had every intention of conquering cancer, even though the doctor who made the initial diagnosis gave my mom only six months to a year to live. While my mom was going through her first course of chemotherapy, we read everything we could about lung cancer, clinical trials, and different therapies. We also planned for the worst-case scenario. We investigated affordable housing and special needs trusts using a network of autism advocates derived from our volunteer work with several autism organizations.

The chemotherapy didn't work. The tumor was not only grow-ing, but it was spreading. Also, my mom was having trouble breath-ing, and she was in excruciating pain. Through my psychiatrist at the

Lurie Center for Autism which is a satellite of Massachusetts General Hospital (MGH), we learned about a clinical trial being conducted by a well-respected MGH oncologist. Ironically, right before my mom was diagnosed, we had participated in an autism drug trial focus group in which the topic of cancer and clinical trials came up. One of the other autism parents had shared how her life had been saved by participating in a clinical trial when she had had a cancer scare a few years earlier. From our own research, we gleaned that when it came to cancer, clinical trials were the way to go, particularly those that used immunotherapy. Immunotherapy was a new field that showed great promise. Immunotherapy drugs had been FDA-approved for certain cancers and were being actively tested in others. As my mom's MGH oncologist put it, "immunotherapy doesn't work most of the time, but when it works, it works really well."

So, my mom enrolled in a clinical trial in which she would be given chemotherapy and immunotherapy. Participating in the clinical trial meant traveling into Boston every three weeks from our home in Bedford, Massachusetts. But my mom's cancer had already changed the tenor of our lives. When we went grocery shopping, my mom always needed to use the wheelchair carts, which meant that I had to push her while she directed where to go. We sometimes laughed at the impression we must have been making on our fellow shoppers. "Why is this woman bossing around this grown man?" As my mother's energy decreased, there were more things I had to do. While I had always helped with household chores and meal prep, the number of tasks I took on increased as my mother stepped further into the background providing verbal prompts and reminders, since I did tend to become forgetful, particularly when under stress. I also had to make frequent trips to the local CVS to pick up my mom's pain medication.

I became my mom's caretaker, and the implications went beyond the simple student becoming the teacher role reversal. My mom was teaching me how best to take care of her. And, in a unique twist, when my autism needed to be considered, it wasn't because I was the patient it was because I was the closest family member of the patient. For instance, since I didn't drive, I was allowed to stay in the hospital with my mom even though I needed no medical care. But regardless of who was taking care of who, or who was doing the teaching, or who was doing the learning, my mom and I were a team just as we had always been my entire life. It was now my turn to be there for her as she had always been there for me.

Chapter One: Inklings

My mother remembers watching the old television show *Mission: Impossible* when she went into labor with me. I was born some 19 hours later, May 5, 1973, in Berkeley, California. My estimated time of arrival was 3:05 pm; a nurse had forgotten to record the exact time of birth. Other than that minor mishap, everything seemed to be going perfectly. I cried immediately, and I scored a 10 on my APGAR. But then, three days later, I was reported to have had a seizure and turned blue—I was subsequently rushed by ambulance from Alta-Bates to Children's Hospital. Later, I would be diagnosed with "minimal brain dysfunction."

Though I have no memory of this period of my life, the four years I lived in Berkeley were, nonetheless, formative and eventful. For one thing, the unevenness of my early development led to me being diagnosed both mentally retarded and gifted in the space of a few short months. One thing was clear, however, the disruptiveness of my behavior rendered remaining in pre-school—even a permissive one like Montessori in a progressive city like Berkeley—impossible.

I grew up in Beverly Hills, but I was not among the wealthy. When my mother and I relocated to Los Angeles after I'd been evaluated at UCLA, she'd been advised that the Beverly Hills Unified School District (BHUSD) had some of the best public schools in California. So, sleeping in the living room of a one-bedroom apartment became one of my mother's first sacrificial offerings to my education.

We weren't rich, but I didn't feel poor. I didn't want for much. My mother and her parents saw to that, but living in Southern California, a part of me couldn't help but wish I had a swimming pool. Several of my classmates enjoyed that privilege, and, at a pool party at one of their houses when I was around 7 years old, my excitement led to me almost drowning. I was perfectly aware that I didn't know how to swim, I, nonetheless, followed the rest of my classmates and jumped into the deep end. The only thing I recall is vomiting chlorine on the smooth, sunbaked terracotta tiles.

Incidentally, this was not my first near-death experience with a swimming pool; almost drowning constitutes my earliest complete memory. I was four years old and visiting my father in Beverly Hills. My mother and I were still living in Berkeley at the time, and my father, who my mother divorced when I was two, had recently married the singer Freda Payne who owned a swimming pool. One moment I am floating on an inflatable raft. The next, I am dangling just beneath the water's surface. I don't remember being scared, though I can still hear myself grunting as I struggle to hold my breath. I can still feel the prickle of the bubbles in the wake of my splash, but what mesmerizes me the most is the color, an all-encompassing turquoise blue that I find pleasant and appealing. I have fallen into a beautiful, cloudless sky, but before I can fully appreciate the canvass, a dark splotch appears before me, and I immediately recognize the figure of a woman in a bathing suit. As my head emerges from the water, my stepmother's face comes clearly into focus.

The circumstances surrounding this memory are as unusual as the memory itself. On the day of my almost drowning, my father had left me in the care of his mother, his new wife, and their maid. Of the adults assembled around the pool that day, my stepmother was the only one who knew how to swim, so even though she was eight months pregnant, she had no choice but to jump into the pool when my grandmother's scream alerted her to the empty raft.

My half-brother was born a month later, leading to yet another anomaly. He was named Gregory Joel Abbott, Jr., after our father, even though I was the firstborn. My mother had wanted me to be a junior, but my father objected to giving me what he, at the time, called a "slave name." My mother consulted a book and came up with Gyasi, a Ghanaian name that means "the wonderful one," a name that I think suits me far better than Gregory—not so much for its meaning but for its uniqueness. Perhaps it's just as well that I was not named after my father since after my parents divorced, I had little contact with him or his relations. My birth certificate reads "Gyasi Omari Burks-Abbott," but as far as I was concerned, I was a Burks.

Growing up, my family consisted of my mother, her two sisters, and their parents. I lived with my mother in California, and I visited my grandparents in New York during holidays and summer vacations. Most of my time I spent with my mother, a graduate student with expertise in film and literature. I enjoyed the endless hours of conversation we would have. I loved listening to my mother analyze movies, television shows, interpersonal relationships, and current events. Unaware of the unique education I was receiving, I was just having a great time.

My mother was the smartest person I knew. In addition to having an exceptionally high I.Q.--an I.Q. so high my grandmother was advised never to reveal it--critical thinking came to my mother like the perennial leaf to a deciduous tree. Even at a young age, I felt that my mother's judgment was the only judgment I could really trust. That's not to say I never disagreed with her, but I often put off forming an opinion until I had an opportunity to run things by her. Even when other adults tried to tell me how the world worked, I always wanted a second opinion—my mother's opinion. While I may not have been an intellectual giant myself, I was all too often amazed at how shortsighted other adults were, particularly those who pretended they possessed all the answers. As far as I was concerned, mommy knew best.

Every summer, we'd visit my grandparents in New York City. I loved flying on airplanes as well as traveling to different places, and my family circumstances provided plenty of opportunities for both. My mother frequently flew to attend conferences and to present papers, and she always took me with her. My grandfather, a bio-chemist who had lost his leg in World War II, was an active member of the Disabled American Veterans' (DAV), and he would take my grandmother and me to the DAV conventions held in a different US city annually. It was at a DAV convention in Miami where I finally learned how to swim when I was about 8 years old. Although I retain no recollection of Miami, the lesson I took from my swim-ming instruction remains indelibly planted in my brain. As soon as I learned to conquer my fear of the water and comprehend that if I didn't panic, my body would float naturally, I took to swimming like a fish to water. Incidentally, not panicking and going with the flow is a life lesson I still strive to internalize.

A major highlight of my summer vacation was the airplane trip. I looked forward to the six-hour flight across the country. The nov-elty of floating in midair and looking down on an altered landscape matched my anticipation of getting to see my grandparents. As I got older, I relished the sense of independence I derived from taking the trip by myself. My fascination with the journey was reflected in the way I misinterpreted the song "New York, New York." For me, the line "if you can make it there, you'll make it anywhere" referred to the fact that New York was the furthest distance you could travel in the continental United States.

My first solo flight was from Oakland to San Diego, and it was not smooth, though, perhaps, fortunately, I remember none of it. My paternal grandparents were convinced that I was old enough to fly alone, even though I was still two months shy of my fifth birthday. Despite having divorced my father, my mother still preferred that I grow up with two responsible parents and two sets of doting grandparents, so she acquiesced; it was less than a 30-minute flight.

She never discovered what happened. After giving me a big hug, strapping me into my seat, and providing the flight attendant with the information regarding who would be meeting me at the other end, my mother disembarked and waited at the gate until she saw the plane taxi onto the runway. The phone was ringing when she returned home. A representative from Pacific Southwest Airlines—"the world's friendliest airline"—politely requested that she come back to the airport and pick me up. When my mother arrived at the gate, she found me playing with the airline employee charged with taking care of me, who also had no idea what had occurred. Once the captain, who apparently felt that the flight could not continue with me onboard, turned the plane around and brought me back, he immediately took off. Whether I knew what I had done, I couldn't or wouldn't say.

Whatever happened on my first solo flight was, apparently, not traumatic enough to turn me off flying, and I always looked forward to visiting my maternal grandparents in New York during summer vacations. My trips to New York usually began with a visit to my grandmother's junior high school English class on what was their last day of school. My grandmother didn't drive, so we'd walk and take the subway, a practice that continued throughout my month-long stay. While my grandfather was at work, my grandmother, who prided herself on being a walker, would take me on sojourns across Manhattan. The city I saw from her vantage point always struck me as a strange and alien world, a world significantly different from the one in which I lived.

There was the uniqueness of riding the subway, which didn't exist in Beverly Hills. And even though I lived amidst all the accouterments of any modern city, paved roads, streetlights, honking cars, and glass buildings, an ambiance of airiness, greenery, and wide-open spaces that I never felt in New York City proliferated. For years, I always conceived of New York as being composed completely of concrete, all rough edges, and hard pavement. I would have sworn there were no trees or grass, only crowds, graffiti, and litter.

On the weekends, when my grandfather was off work, he showed me a softer, more scenic side of New York when he drove my grandmother and me upstate to a rustic retreat in Ossining. The place I called "the Lake"—a recreational facility for disabled American veterans replete with ping pong and pool tables, barbecue and picnic areas, and, of course, a lake—had been created so my grandfather and other wounded warriors could enjoy swimming, rowing, and other outdoor activities despite being barred from other public venues due to their disfiguring injuries. Growing up, I was blissfully unaware of the social stigma surrounding "the Lake."

When I started kindergarten at five years old, I was placed in regular classes. I remember stepping on a big black bug, an insignificant event remarkable only because I remember it so vividly. Standing in line on the little playground directly outside the classroom, waiting to be escorted to the main playground downstairs, I can still see the bug's caved-in black body resting on top of its own red stain. I was astounded by the fact that I had just taken a life, that I had been an agent of destiny.

Most of my other memories of kindergarten are vague. I remember my contentious relationship with the Monkey Bars, a dome-shaped, wrought-ironed structure located on the main playground. Monkey wrestling was a recess staple in which the object was to be the last one hanging. There were a few one-on-one matches, but mostly, there were huge hug fests in which a bunch of us would try to pry each other loose with our legs. In one of these mass melees, a pair of human pliers pulled me from the Monkey Bars, and I landed face-first on the padded asphalt-colored mat, losing my two front teeth. When my permanent teeth grew back, they grew back bucked and crooked, and if the classmates who called me "four eyes" because of my eyeglasses had been more original, they could have easily likened me to Alvin the Chipmunk.

One day those same monkey bars knocked me upside the head. The cut was small and shallow, so minuscule, in fact, the band-aid was just a tiny circle, but it was located on the side of my head just where I felt the sensation on my scalp when chewing or swallowing. For several weeks, eating became an annoyingly conscious experience, and I imagined particles of food sticking out of my head behind the adhesive. Eventually, I managed to create a semi-permanent circular bald spot on my temple in obsessive pursuit of the head itch that, I now realize in retrospect, accompanied the healing.

Scratching became a hypnotic activity I engaged in for hours. As focused as I was on getting rid of the itch, I also hoped one day to catch a glimpse of it. When I wasn't holding hair follicles up for close inspection or laying them down on surfaces waiting for the "itch" to manifest itself, I massaged my head with my fingers or parted my hair so I could get directly to the site and rub…and rub…and rub… and rub. I once asked my grandfather what an itch was, and he told me it was a "funny feeling on the skin." I already knew what it felt like; I wanted to know what it looked like. What color was it? How big was it? What was its shape? Though depending on the feeling, I'd imagine lines, squiggles, spots, and flakes, I wasn't satisfied; I needed to see these strange sensations for myself.

Another early memory is of my sixth birthday party. I'd provided my mother with the names of the kids in my class who I wanted to invite, and she'd written them on invitations that I was to ask my Kindergarten teacher to distribute for me. The teacher suggested that I place them into each child's bucket myself, so I did even though I couldn't read. I went around the classroom randomly dropping invitations into buckets while also informing classmates that they were invited to my party. I wound up inviting a lot of kids who I had no intention of asking, and on the day of the party, almost every kid in my class showed up, creating a crowd control problem for my mom.

Fortunately, we lived directly across the street from the elementary school, so my mother was able to contain the crowd by having us spend much of the time playing in the school's playground. While my classmates thought this was the best party ever, towards the end of the day, I began to break down. There were just too many presents, too many decorations, and too much noise. When we played pin the tail on the donkey, I couldn't even find the wall, much less the donkey, and, when my mother broke the piñata, and party favors came streaming out, the hordes of kids flinging themselves on the floor in search of the best ones sent me to crying so hysterically that I had to take a nap before the festivities ended.

Although my mother assures me it's not the case, I used to wonder if my idiotic behavior with the invitations precipitated the recommendation that I be placed in a special day class. The text from my first Individualized Educational Program (IEP) that follows confirms my mother's assurances, but, initially, my mother was as baffled as I, particularly when the special education administrator told her I spoke with the vocabulary of a 40-year-old. In fact, the "discrepancy between intellectual ability and academic achievement in math and letter formation due to a perceptual-motor difficulty," compounded by "difficulties with fine and gross motor skills," provided the rationale for transferring me from Beverly Vista, where I could walk across the street to school to Horace Mann where my mother would have to drive me, at least until we moved within walking distance of the school.

I took it for granted that I was not academically inclined, and I didn't particularly mind. I knew I was nothing like my mother. Whereas she started reading when she was 3 years old and, as a child, preferred reading to watching TV, I didn't begin reading until I was 6 and preferred watching TV. And, in contrast to the "A" average my mother maintained throughout her K-12 years, my school performance was as uneven as a mountain range with peaks and valleys and unfathomable canyons.

In first grade, I was transferred to a special education classroom at Horace Mann with a teacher named, ironically enough, Mrs. Brilliant. The special education class was small and tight-knit; there were never any more than 12 students, and the turnover rate was next to nothing. The class composition was eclectic; the ages ranged from 6-11 years, and the disabilities varied from deafness, speech impediments, learning disabilities, emotional problems, and, evidently, the Autism Spectrum. As a class, we bonded. We played with each other in the schoolyard. Sometimes we separated by gender; Jose would pretend to be The Incredible Hulk because he was big, and Jordan, Robin, Roby, and I would be his fighting fodder; Camie, Ilene, Karen, and Shawn would play hopscotch. Most times, however, we stuck together—we'd swing, we'd slide, and we'd play tag.

As much as I liked Mrs. Brilliant and felt at home in the class, these were not halcyon days. First, there was the pool party at Karen's house, the one I mentioned earlier, where I almost drowned. When I ran into Karen about a decade later, and she failed to remember who I was, I shuddered at the realization that she certainly would never have forgotten me had things turned out differently that day. Then there was the conflict I had with a kid named Taki, who seemed to have a compulsion to pull my glasses off my face and break them. Things came to a head one day when Debbie, one of Mrs. Brilliant's assistants, came to collect us from recess, and Taki, who had just failed in his attempt to snatch my glasses, started to cry, and Debbie immediately embraced him. I don't remember whether I punched, kicked, or pushed, but I do remember being enraged and yelling at both Debbie and Taki. Mrs. Brilliant gave me a "Poor" in behavior, at which point it was my turn to start crying. All sympathy went to Taki, however, because he was new (both to the country as well as the class), and he was soft-spoken and shy. I, on the other hand, while not an outgoing extrovert and generally a nice kid, had a reputation for losing my temper.

When I was partially mainstreamed in 2nd or 3rd grade, I attracted a lot of attention from my non-disabled peers because of my glasses and my braces. My nicknames were "four eyes" and "brace face," and my glasses were frequently stolen and broken. I was also notoriously bad in sports, and my reputation as a "spaze" was also a constant cause for taunting and teasing. As many times as my mother and others told me to ignore my tormentors, I couldn't control my temper. In a scene reminiscent of a bullfight, my peers would form a circle around me and take turns approaching with insults; I'd see red and charge. I'd yell, scream, kick, and curse. Even when my running around the playground triggered my exercise-induced asthma, I still managed to keep going. Rage was my fuel.

Maybe I'd say something that angered someone enough to turn around and head in my direction, or maybe I'd catch someone off guard who thought I was in pursuit of someone else; or maybe I'd be chasing one of the slower members of my jeering section--either way, there was always a fight. Anyone who engaged in hand-to-hand combat with me was always impressed with my strength. I could be tackled, kicked, and punched, but I could not be subdued or stopped. I'd get to a point where I had so much anger that I had to sandwich my lips between my gritting teeth and scream in order to dissipate some of it. At that point, I really didn't feel pain. Every blow just inflamed me more—I was a bonfire being sprinkled with gasoline.

After I was completely mainstreamed in 4th grade and joined a regular homeroom class, I participated in the yearly ritual of making gingerbread houses to enjoy during the holiday break. Unfortunately, my gingerbread house never made it home. As soon as I was done putting my house in order, my classmates would descend upon it like pigeons picking at breadcrumbs in a park. It would begin with a classmate playing a game of "even Steven"--taking a jelly bean from each side of the roof, for instance--claiming to be maintaining a sense of aesthetic balance. Other classmates would join in this balancing act until, by the time I was outside of the school on my way home for the holiday break, my originally ornate, decked-out house looked more like a dilapidated shack. The foundations of the shack would begin to crumble, and the pigeons turned into vultures, picking at the carcass until I dropped it, chased them, and scattered the buzzards with verbal buckshot.

Academic life in special education was boring. Everyone in the class would work independently on their own assignments, which, at least for me, entailed endless hours of rote memorization and recall. Mrs. Brilliant and one of her assistants would supervise us to make sure that our minds didn't wander (as mine usually did) and to answer any questions we might have. At the end of the day, our work was collected, checked for mistakes, and given to us to correct and bring back the following day. We were also given performance evaluations that were to be signed by our parents and returned to Mrs. Brilliant.

Sometimes the class would come together, which to me was synonymous with it coming alive. Whether it was for a general lesson delivered by Mrs. Brilliant, a session of arts-n-crafts, or some other special presentation like when the class was taught how Karen's hearing aid worked; I always appreciated the novelty and the break from routine. Another memory of note is of my introduction to math. The memory is unique because it is a good one. I can still recall Debbie introducing me to multiplication and praising me when I answered a question correctly. After that, I only remember being notoriously bad in math and hating the subject with a passion.

According to my mother, I was once good in math and only began on a downward spiral when I was partially mainstreamed and deemed to be stronger in English. Unfortunately, I have no memory of this. I only remember the literal pain in the neck of tedious arithmetic and my making stupid mistakes because I couldn't keep my columns straight. I also remember the unpleasant smell and feel of pencil lead on my fingers as well as the annoying presence of eraser debris which combined with my squiggly scroll, made my work illegible. My mind would often wander, focusing, at times, on the reflection of the perforations in the ceiling cast on the glass face of my digital watch.

Math became a nuisance and a bore, as ambition numbing as it was soul-crushing. I spent my days churning out numbers with no concept as to why it was important or even interesting. Math was just something I had to do. To my mother's chagrin, I had a mantra I'd chant from time to time in a rhythmic monotone. In slow motion, I'd repeat over and over again, "I reeeally don't feeeel up to doooing maaath, but I haaave to do maaath." I'd indulge in this chant whether confronted with a math assignment or not because I liked the way it felt and sounded. I enjoyed trying to see how slow and low I could go and for how long I could stretch out the word "math." I did this the entire time I was in special education between 1st and 3rd grade.

While the general understanding was that I had some kind of learning disability, some of my teachers interpreted my situation less charitably; they felt that I was not applying myself and would chastise me for being slow and lazy. My 5th-grade science teacher even went so far as to write "a mind is a terrible thing to waste" (quoting what was then the slogan for the United Negro College Fund) across the top of an exam in which I'd failed the math portion.

Though completely mainstreamed by 4th grade, I still spent an hour a day in what was called the Resource Room with Mrs. Brown.

The Resource Room was structured more like a tutoring center than like a class; students would come in at different times and work independently. Mrs. Brown would give us assignments based on our grade and skill level, and there were always at least two assistants at any one time supervising and answering questions.

I started out with Mrs. Brown doing both reading and math. I divided my time between children's books and math problems--neither coming to any avail. I was not learning how to read, and my math scores were plummeting. My mother finally succeeded in teaching me how to read by using some books from her job at an organization called Educational Insights. She also put labels around the house indicating what different objects were and a magnetic alphabet set on the refrigerator for me to play with.

As my mother tells it, one night, I read a children's book with ease. She took me in to show the school that I no longer needed Resource for reading. Unfortunately, the school officials didn't believe her; they insisted that I must have memorized the book. They gave me another children's book to read and, eventually, it was agreed that I did, in fact, know how to read. Now the trick was to get me interested in reading. My mother planted the seeds that would eventually flower into a love of reading by encouraging me to explore my interests in American history and biography. She bought me a subscription to American History Magazine and a set of Funk & Wagnall's Encyclopedias, the latter which I would spend hours perusing (this was before Google) looking up facts about famous people. I was also a regular participant in the Beverly Hills Public Library summer reading program.

When it came to doing schoolwork, I always needed a lot of help from my mother, a situation that I thought was unique to me but one I have since learned is quite common in school-aged children. I got a brief glimpse of this reality in fourth grade when I was confronted by a particularly taxing vocabulary assignment. We were given fifty vocabulary words to look up, define, and use in a sentence. The only thing I remember from that assignment is my mother's refrain, "It has to be on this page!" as she was trying to teach me how to use the dictionary. It's not a painful memory. In fact, "it has to be on this page!" is a self-stim I sometimes entertain myself with to this day.

Anyway, my mother was suspicious of how much difficulty I had in completing the assignment, so she spoke with some other parents. It turned out that I was not the only student who was up all night with a parent, and the teacher was forced to apologize and promise to reduce the number of future homework assignments. But homework would remain a challenge for me throughout school, and I would require a great deal of assistance from my mother. I had particular difficulty with planning and executing long-range projects.

I was also very accident-prone. When I wasn't in the vice-principal's office for fighting, I was in the nurse's office because I had knocked my head against something. The injuries were never serious, just knots on the head that needed an icepack. Bumping into things, like slides or swings, and going to the nurse's office to pick up an ice pack became an almost daily ritual.

It was in the nurse's office where I realized I had finally figured out how to read a watch. There had been a false positive a few months earlier when, after looking at my watch, I rushed into Mrs. Brown's classroom, apologizing for being late only to have her look at me quizzically and say, "But you're fifteen minutes early." On this occasion in the nurse's office, I remember following the second hand while my temperature was being taken and noting 20 minutes had passed when, to my pleasant surprise, the nurse said, "Oh, Gyasi, I'm sorry. I left that thing in your mouth for 20 minutes." She hadn't just read my mind; I could tell time! But, alas, this would turn out to be a flash in the pan as another 30 years would pass before I felt comfortable using an analog instead of a digital watch.

But I was patient. My love of history afforded me a rich mental life that countered many of my problems in the present. Biographies of people who struggled but eventually made good offered me hope, and accounts of historical turning points provided me with excitement. When I would learn about the explorers of the New World or events from the American Revolution, I always tried to imagine what the past looked like and felt like. I once even asked my mother if color existed back when she was a child. In retrospect, I realize just how much that question was inspired by black-and-white archival footage from the 1950s of my mother's youth since I never doubted that color existed in any other era. But still, I wondered what it would be like to experience the past, travel back in time, and witness a historical event. I would sometimes entertain myself by re-enacting narratives I'd heard in history class.

I was a generally happy child, and looking back, I feel I had a good childhood. However, I did tend to see my life as half-empty. My mother introduced me to creative visualization, a tool I would use to imagine a better life for myself. In one rather silly scenario, I would visualize my classmates chanting my name after variations of who's the greatest, i.e., smartest, fastest, and strongest. Outside of creative visualization, I had my own version of an afterlife. I always relished the possibility that the descendants of the kids who made fun of me would be reading about me in school.

When I wasn't re-enacting historical events, I would cast myself as the protagonist in an action/adventure movie. I had this quality I referred to as "being good at it," which meant I could hang from speeding vehicles, clear wide canyons, and run through explosions with little effort. I had this ongoing narrative of classmates trying to kill me but always failing because of my physical agility.

I loved cats, but I was allergic to cat dander. I loved to run, but I had exercised-induced asthma. Fortunately, my imaginary friend was a cat who ran with the speed and grace of an Olympian so that I could experience the joys of running and the company of a cat without risking an asthma or allergy attack. My imaginary cat was a ghost (hence, his invisibility) of a real cat that had achieved another one of my fantasies—life until 110-years-old. Why 110? I loved even numbers, particularly those ending with zeroes, and the number 10 was my favorite. When I was 10-ten-years old, I creatively visualized living another 100 years. By the time I turned 11, I had figured that I had cosmically committed myself to die in 2083, my 110th year. At least, that's how I remember it.

My mother identified another possible origin for my 110-year-old imaginary cat. She reminded me about the palm-reader, a family friend, who introduced me to the concept of a lifeline. I remember the lifeline—it was a subject of fascination for me for years—but I had forgotten where I had learned about it. Anyway, according to my mother, the palm reader predicted, based on my lifeline, that I would live to be 110 years old. The only thing I can remember about my visit to the palm reader's house was being reduced to sneezing and nose blowing by her very real cat.

Another subject that captured my imagination was French. My mother had spent three months in France a year before I was born, and she sometimes spoke French to me when I was a baby. France took on almost mythic proportions for me; I imagined a place devoid of the usual American prejudices, where outsiders like me could easily fit in. I was inspired by the tales of expatriates like Richard Wright and James Baldwin, African American authors who migrated to France in search of equality.

A major wish of mine was to spend a year in France. Many of my classmates were from other countries, and I wanted to see the world from their perspective. I wondered what it was like to be in a strange land interacting in a foreign tongue. I figured it must be exciting, and I wanted to experience it for myself. My first best friend, other than my mother, was a French kid named Cedric, who

I'd met in 5th grade when I started taking French. We met on the first day of class, and I remember our first interaction. Excited at the opportunity to try my French on a real French person, I asked Cedric in French if he spoke French. After humming out loud and bouncing on his desk for a few seconds, he responded in English, "Yes, I do."

Cedric and I were both outsiders. Cedric was new to Horace Mann, and, like me, he wore glasses and was a loner. We'd hang out by ourselves at recess, and we'd do things together after school like play video games or go to the Beverly Center Mall. Our friendship attracted some negative attention--it was another thing that my class-mates decided to hold against me. I once got a prank call from some kid saying, "Gyasi loves Cedric," before hanging up. Cedric was just as unpopular as I was, and I got into one of my bullfights running an errand for him. Cedric was in love with Shannon, one of the most popular girls in the school, and he wanted to know how he ranked among her other two suitors, David and Bryan. Cedric sent me to find out.

Shannon told me that she liked David and Bryan better than Cedric. I remember being surprised that Shannon would be so open about who she liked. I responded, "Oh! So, you like David and Bryan?" Shannon, who had been talking to two other girls when I approached, was already annoyed by my presence, and my query didn't make me any more palatable. She corrected me, "No! I said I liked Bryan and David better than Cedric. Now, get out of here, Gyasi." On my way back from Shannon, I was set upon by a group of kids who wanted to play "keep away" with my hat. As expected, I chased them back and forth, up and down, and all around the play-ground, trapped in their game like a laboratory rat.

Cedric was a misfit. He loved pranks and practical jokes like stuffing paper in the tops of saltshakers. He taught me how to litter without getting caught--just let whatever is in your hand fall while walking normally. He showed me a little trick that could guarantee victory in any fight--or, at least, ensure a fighting chance; raise your hand to strike and, once you've got your opponent focusing on your fist, kick them with your foot.

Cedric was also a kleptomaniac, and, unfortunately for many shopkeepers, he was good at it too. Cedric was so smooth and subtle that I was usually unaware he had stolen until after the fact; we'd walk out of the store and, Cedric would show me what he had taken. Once, Cedric asked a jeweler for the price of a gold chain, thanked her, walked out of the store with it, and gave it to his mother for Mother's Day. Cedric was like a professional; he'd been shoplifting for years, and he had only been caught once--in France. In the United States, Cedric had never been caught.

My mother worried that if Cedric ever did get caught, I, being black, would be the one who got in trouble. She admonished me that while I may not be able to stop Cedric from stealing, I should make sure he didn't steal around me. But Cedric was unstoppable--he kept walking out of stores pulling stuff out of his pockets like a magician. The only thing I could do was to keep our shopping trips to a minimum.

Ironically, I was once accused of stealing with a friend, but from a store that I had never even shopped at with Cedric. It was the neighborhood Ralph's Supermarket, and I was taking one of my first trips alone to pick up some groceries. While standing in line, one of the store managers asked me, "How's the cart thief?" I thought he was joking, and even though I didn't get the joke, I smiled out of politeness. The man standing behind me said, "Yeah, he's the one." I started to feel very self-conscious, and my face began to form my trademark Idiot Grin.

The Idiot Grin was a distorted smile caused by my left cheek slowly moving upwards. I couldn't control it. My only defense was to try and hide it. Sometimes I'd get lucky. An uncomfortable situation would occur while I was sitting, and all I would have to do was rest the left side of my face on my hand. But when I was standing, like I was that day in Ralph's, there was nothing I could do. Fighting the Grin only made it worse—I'd look as ridiculous as someone trying to control his or her mouth after it has been numbed with Lidocaine.

I don't remember exactly what happened next. I was just happy to get out of the store. When I got home, I told my mother about this strange thing that had happened while I was shopping. To my surprise, my mother was furious and immediately placed a call to Ralph's. The only thing I remember about that conversation was my mother yelling, apparently in response to something the manager said, "What? No Retribution?"

It turns out I couldn't have misread the situation more if I had thought I was being anointed Shopper of the Year. The manager's quip "How's the cart thief?" was not a joke or some sort of bizarre greeting; it was an accusation, and my enigmatic smile was seen as a confession. Apparently, I looked just like some black kid who had stolen some carts from the parking lot with a friend about a week earlier. But the manager had no hard feelings, and he wasn't going to press any charges.

Beverly Hills was a small community that didn't have many black people; I pretty much knew all the other black kids in the entire school district. I wondered who the real culprit could be. Fortunately, I was at a doctor's appointment at the time of the crime, so I had an alibi. This did not stop the manager from making Ralph's a very uncomfortable shopping environment for my mother and me despite his claims of forgiveness and no hard feelings. It would take the intervention of a lawyer friend of my mother's, who confronted the manager and demanded he either press charges or lay off, stop the dirty looks and subtle surveillance. As far as I know, the real cart thieves were never caught.

Chapter Two: Irony 101

When I was 11 years old in 5th grade, I became the target of Luther, the neighborhood bully, which indirectly led to me being almost diagnosed autistic, a circumstance my mom once referred to as both a misdiagnosis and missed diagnosis. I'd add it was also a missed moment, like when two people who are destined to get together cross paths without realizing it. Luther lived on the farthest end of my block, and I had to pass by his house in order to get to school. Almost every day, on my way to or from school, Luther suddenly appeared. He'd emerge from the palm trees flanking both sides of the sidewalk and set upon me like we were in the wild. He was the predator, and I was his prey. He'd taunt me, tease me, and threaten to kill me—emphasizing the latter point with punches and kicks. I began to refer to that portion of Hamilton Drive as "Death Row."

One day, Luther gave me a pretty good sock in the jaw—one of the few times in my life I can remember being injured in a physical altercation. My face was red and sore, and I was sure something must be broken. I felt relief when my mother assured me that a break would have caused a lot more pain. Most of my encounters with Luther occurred on that little stretch of the street at the end of our block. One of the few times Luther attacked me at school, he was joined by some of the usual kids who liked to pick on me, which might be why, in this case, I felt empowered to fight back. All of us wound up in the Vice-Principal's office.

Even though I was a lot smaller than Luther, the Vice-Principal accused me of being the instigator in my run-ins with this far larger boy. My reputation for fighting gave me a credibility problem, and the fact that I was seeing a school counselor cemented my designation as a problem child. Though usually low-key, and optimistic, I was also given to acting out in bouts of angry depression. There was the time while sitting in Mrs. Brilliant's class, where apropos of nothing; I announced, "I wish I was dead." Then there was that more passionate display of rage and despair whose melodrama still makes me cringe. I had just recovered from an asthma attack, attacks that were becoming more frequent and severe now that the class was running track every day. Half-heartedly, almost as if going through the motions of some pathetic persona, I confronted a female classmate with my suspicions that she was not really my friend but merely felt sorry for me.

Thanks, in part, to my less than stellar conduct my mother was my only initial ally when it came to Luther. When I was referred to Cedars-Sinai for psychiatric treatment, advanced notice was sent that I was a troublemaker, a warning my psychiatrist, Dr. Brody, really took to heart. Not only were my reports of Luther's harassment greeted with skepticism but also Dr. Brody felt that my problems in math were the result of pure laziness. During one session, she put her foot down and insisted I complete some math problems right there in her office. Still traumatized later that night, my mother had me call Dr. Brody's emergency number, and the latter apologized for her own behavior. While waiting for Dr. Brody to call me back, my mother had me call my grandmother in New York, who helped talk me down from my psychic ledge with an important piece of enduring wisdom which I'll paraphrase "It is more important to do a job correctly than quickly."

Dr. Brody's attitude towards me began to change after a chance encounter with a colleague at a staff meeting. It turned out that Luther was also a patient at Cedars-Sinai, and he'd often brag to his therapist about the small boy he was bullying, giving details that confirmed everything I told Dr. Brody. It also turned out that I was not Luther's first victim, and the Vice-Principal who tried to place the blame squarely on me was perfectly aware of his history, which included a police record. In speaking to the police as well as the parents of some of Luther's other victims, my mother discovered that Luther was a serial bully who had a type (light-skinned black boys like himself), and the Vice-Principal had a financial reason to ignore the threat that Luther posed to other students. Acknowledging that Luther had emotional problems would require the school district to pay for private school.

Then there was the Vice Principal's own racism demonstrated by her unfair administering of discipline to black and white students. In a particularly egregious case, the Vice Principal suspended a black student for engaging in an act of self-defense—he kicked a knife out of the hand of a white student. After my mother filed a formal complaint against Luther with the police, they arrested him at school in order to force the Vice Principal to act, which she did by suspending Luther temporarily. As a result of Horace Mann's lenient treatment of Luther and unsympathetic attitude towards me, it was thought best that I transfer back to Hawthorne, a school I had attended in 2nd grade when my special education class moved from Horace Mann to Hawthorne, stayed there for a year, before moving back to Horace Mann.

At the time, I processed the move as simply me no longer having to cross "Death Row" since Hawthorne was in the opposite direction of Horace Mann. Though on one of my last trips down that part of the street, I ran into an apologetic Luther who offered to beat anyone up who messed with me. All the same, just like when I was moved from Beverly Vista to Horace Mann, I once again went from a school within walking distance from my house to one in which I'd need a ride. This time, however, my mother was able to teach me how to take the bus.

After transferring to Hawthorne, I continued to see Dr. Brody, who had resigned her position as a counselor for the school district (in protest for the way I had been treated) and had gone into private practice. Dr. Brody began to suspect that I might be autistic. I don't know what made her think so, but I do remember the time when she offered me a piece of candy, and I stuck my hand in the bowl and grabbed a whole bunch. After reviewing a tape of one of our sessions, Dr. Ornitz, an autism expert at UCLA, concurred with Dr. Brody's conclusion that I showed signs of autism. I was subsequently tested by another autism specialist, Dr. BJ Freeman, who incidentally was the same doctor who had diagnosed me mentally retarded when I was 3 1/2-years old.

Fortunately, my mother never accepted the diagnosis of mental retardation, and her doubts were vindicated by an evaluation by a neurologist named Dr. Umansky, who found me to be...well, I remember being told as a child that the diagnosis was gifted while working on this book my mom told me the diagnosis was genius. Either way, when my mother asked for an explanation for the discrepancy between mental retardation and superior mental functioning, Dr. Umansky responded eloquently, "While one can never perform above their potential, they can always perform below it." When my mother went back to Dr. Freeman and contested the diagnosis of mental retardation, it came to light that I had been suffering from an ear infection during the testing.

Fast forward to me at 11; Dr. Freeman now felt that I had once been autistic but was currently in remission. The official diagnosis was Autism-Residual State. There was no therapy or treatment for someone at my level of functioning. Dr. Freeman felt that my mother had been doing a great job and should just continue doing what she was doing.

What was my mother doing?

With no special diets to follow, my mother simply fed me based on her own understanding of good nutrition. My mother was a big believer in the health benefits of eating fresh food, so we rarely ate frozen or fast food. My mother also felt that the best diet should include a little bit of everything, so I was exposed to a variety of types of foods from a young age. One dietary restriction I had was sugar. The restriction wasn't absolute; I could eat cake at birthday parties or dessert at restaurants, but on the rare occasions when I did consume sugar at home, it was of the health food variety like lemon-lime soda or tiger's milk bars. I also took vitamin supplements every day.

With no social skills classes to enroll me in, my mother simply taught me what she knew and let me know what type of behavior she did and did not approve of. As a graduate student, my mother had to travel a lot to academic conferences, and as a single parent, she was forced to take me with her. I was exposed to a variety of social interactions in several different contexts as a result. I also enjoyed the comradery of classmates, some of whom I'd also interact with at after-school Day Care. There was Justin, who loved to dress up in camouflage and pretend to be a soldier; he always included me in his war games. There was Brian, who loved to make popping sounds by slapping his cheeks with his mouth open. Brian and I both loved silly talk, and one night, to my delight but my mother's chagrin, he left a gibberish-laden message on our answering machine. Looking back, I wonder if Brian might have been on the Autism Spectrum. And there was Tony and Jason, two of the only other black students at Horace Mann, who introduced me to the Cub Scouts, which led to my lifelong association with the Boy Scouts.

Indeed, I was basically a normal kid who had normal childhood experiences, and my problems were dealt with in normal ways. There were no autism-oriented special programs or self-help books. When my mother wanted me to learn martial arts so that I could defend myself if I ever encountered another Luther, she enrolled me in Tae Kwon Do classes at a local studio. When my mother wanted me to have a male role model to fill in the gap left by my absentee father, there was the Big Brothers of Greater Los Angeles. And, when my mother wanted to encourage me to pursue Scouting, she volunteered as a troop committee chair, bringing her organizational skills to bear in making sure the troop ran as efficiently as possible.

Incidentally, Boy Scouts gave me a sense of competence and importance. It was a place where I could distinguish myself while learning important skills. For some reason, I found myself less reserved and better able to handle the social dynamics of my Boy Scout troop. It was almost like I became a different person. I always regretted that my teachers and classmates could not see me in the context of my Boy Scout troop. I resolved this problem by conjuring an image of my classmates and teachers watching me while I was doing Boy Scout stuff.

The closest real encounter between my Boy Scout life and my school life came when I was chosen to participate in the "City Government for a Day" program in which Boy Scouts from different troops spent a day with members of the Beverly Hills Mayor's cabinet. There was a very official-looking picture of me in the local paper. I am wearing my uniform and sitting behind a desk in the Mayor's office with a serious expression on my face.

The program took place on a school day which meant that I had to tell my teachers where I was going to be, and, of course, some of my classmates would be curious as to where I had been. This was a fortuitous opportunity to talk about my achievements without ostensibly bragging. Though, I guess I did have some bragging rights. Since transferring to Hawthorne, I was doing quite well. I was managing the bus by myself, I was making friends, and I even made the honor roll.

My main coterie of friends was a group of outsiders named Leeron, Shalom, and Eran. Eran was a mediocre student, but Leeron and Shalom were classic nerds who used big words, did well in school, and were so laden down with facts that they were always dropping them. Leeron even added to the persona by being a dead ringer for Star Trek's Captain Spock. Even though I had academic successes, I sometimes felt like the black sheep of the group. My uneven profile of abilities confused me as much as it did my teachers. No one seemed able to account for why I was so good in some things and terrible in others. As I mentioned, the going theory was that I had some type of learning disability; though some of my teachers, like the one who wrote "A mind is a terrible thing to waste" across the top of one of my papers, were far harsher in their assessments.

But if I was the black sheep of my little group, the group itself was the black sheep of the entire school. The social scene at Hawthorne was a lot like the set of an interactive soap opera with the Popular Group being center stage, perpetually engaged in romantic intrigue, while the rest of the school, the studio audience, looked on with interest and envy. Though relegated to the studio audience, I was in a section that often got scanned by the camera. My propensity for falling in love with unattainable girls (which pretty much included all girls) and talking about it attracted a lot of attention.

History repeated itself over and over again. I would get excited, and even though I knew better (how many times had my mother warned me?), I'd confide in someone about my latest crush, and they would intercede (with or without my permission) by telling the subject of my affections of her new status. The school would erupt in a tabloid-like frenzy, and after my fifteen minutes of shame, any friendly ties I might have hoped to achieve with the girl in question would be severed forever. I once even got a thinly veiled threat. A girl named Ali was pretending to like me, and she was presenting a very interesting case. Sometimes Ali made it clear that she was playing some sort of game; she'd tell me that the boy she liked had a name that began with the letter "G" and sounded like "Gyasi." Other times, she was a bit more subtle. So subtle, in fact, that I almost missed it. Once I ran into Ali at the Beverly Center Mall, and she was with another boy; later that evening, she called me to say that the boy I had seen her with was not the one she liked. My mom thought that Ali's calling me was unnecessary and, therefore, quite interesting.

I had no interest in Ali, but I liked the idea of being the possible object of female desire, and I also welcomed the mental challenge of trying to figure her out. My juvenile attraction went to a girl named Mona Lisa, who Ali, acting as my messenger and informant, assured me only liked me as a friend. Even though I didn't trust Ali, her assessment of the situation made sense to me, so I accepted it. Then another classmate turned to me in class one day and told me that Mona Lisa liked me more than just as a friend. I was skeptical but figured there would be no harm in checking it out, so I sent Eran on a mission to see Mona Lisa. As I suspected, the classmate had lied.

What I hadn't anticipated was the nasty note I got from Mona Lisa saying that she hated me and warning that if I ever broached the topic of liking her again, she would do something that I could not "deceive." To add to my everlasting humiliation, my mother had to help me formulate a response, and the only sentence I remember from that note is the one informing Mona Lisa that the word is "conceive," not "deceive."

A crush I had on a girl named Pamela led to an encounter with Monica Lewinski, the future First Mistress central to the impeachment of President Bill Clinton. Even though Pamela had once called me stupid when I acted clumsily in a cooking class, I looked at her one day and decided I was in love with her. I wrote a note to Pamela letting her know how I felt and asking her if she wanted to be my girlfriend. Pamela responded with a note telling me that she thought I was a nice person but that she could not date until she was 16 years old.

As many times as I swore to myself that I would keep my feelings for Pamela a secret, I didn't, and my classmates took this latest emotional indiscretion as an opportunity to interrogate me. My appearance before the Committee to Figure Out Gyasi, a jury of my peers lined up against the lockers grilling me about who I liked, is a bit of a blur. But my one conversation with Monica Lewinski, which stemmed from my bid for the class presidency, is quite clear.

Even though my flirtation with a presidential run was short-lived, the fact that I had considered it quickly became common knowledge. A couple of months after my exit from public life, Monica Lewinski approached me and attempted to tantalize me with a behind-the-scenes look into her own campaign for school office. According to Monica, Pamela let it slip during an argument that she was in love with me. Supposedly, Pamela had threatened to resign as Monica's campaign manager and become mine.

It was at Hawthorne that I got into my last fist fight, and the kid I got into a fight with was of glitterati lineage, Damon Elliot, the son of singer Dionne Warwick. I don't remember what the fight was about or even who won though I do recall Damon telling someone how surprisingly strong I was for a person my size. Not only was Damon a lot bigger than me, but also he had a red belt in Tae Kwon Do which is two degrees under a black belt and several degrees above my yellow belt.

"He could have massacred you!" Mr. Ubick, the principal, said with anger and concern as Damon and I sat in his office. Mr. Ubick put us on detention and tasked us with discussing what had happened and coming up with a way for it never to happen again--he wanted it in writing by five o'clock when the school closed. Damon and I only spent a few minutes working on the actual write-up, but if what

Mr. Ubick wanted was for Damon and me to part on good terms, we really spent the entire hour and a half of detention achieving the principle of the assignment. Damon and I lost track of time as we engaged in juvenile male bonding and raunchy adolescent humor. At a few minutes to five, we finally got down to business. The very next year, Damon and I would, once again, find our paths crossing in front of Mr. Ubick's desk, except, this time, Mr. Ubick would be dealing with Damon's governess, my mother, and a racist teacher.

The eighth-grade history teacher was a mass of contradictions. Her last name was Frischman, but because she didn't like the fact that her name ended with the word "man," she insisted that the class spell her name with a "y," Frischmyn. The class further accommodated her by referring to her as Frischwoman and Frischperson. However, when it came to the "All Men are Created Equal" in the Declaration of Independence, Ms. Frischman made it a point to remind the class that the "Men" was simply generic.

Ms. Frischman further confounded with her allocation of points for the weekly "People from the Past" assignment, in which we had to look up information about different historical figures. In Ms. Frischman's breakdown, as my mother once pointed out, the more work you had to do to find out about a person, the fewer points you earned. White males were worth 3 points, white females were worth 2 points, and both black males and females were worth 1 point.

A disdain for African Americans was the only discernable pattern behind Ms. Frischman's behavior. She would say the word "black" as if it left a bad taste in her mouth, and she created a black face exhibition. I didn't know what blackface was, and I thought it only natural that someone else be chosen to play the lead role in the reenactment of the court case involving the slave Dred Scott. Wasn't I always the last chosen—why should it be any different in the classroom than it was on the playground? But when I got home from school on the day of the actual skit, and I told my mother about how the white kid playing Dred Scott had brown make-up smeared all over his face, she introduced me to the history of minstrelsy.

For another one of Ms. Frischman's history skits, my mother took the opportunity to give me a more nuanced view of history than I would ever get from my narrow-minded teacher. My mother helped me construct a controversial character--the brother of Thomas Jefferson's slave lover, Sally Hemings. In the actual skit, I was simply a quadroon doctor; in the write-up, I handed in to Ms. Frischman, I revealed my complete identity. Ms. Frischman was furious, but I don't remember any negative response from her other than the exhortation she wrote on my paper for me to stop telling lies.

When a DNA test later confirmed that Thomas Jefferson fathered at least one of Sally Hemings' children, too many years had passed for me to care enough to feel vindicated though I did appreciate the irony. It put me in mind of the story I once heard about the law student who challenged his score on an exam when his assessment of a hypothetical scenario marked incorrect by the professor was proven true by a subsequent ruling in an actual case. If there was any vindication, it was an affirmation of the confidence my mother tried to instill in me to always think critically, even in the face of authority.

Inevitably, my mother and Ms. Frischman wound up having a parent-teacher conference, and it turned out that there were zeros next to my name for assignments I had turned in. My mother, Damon's governess, and the parents of Brian and his twin brother Mark met with Mr. Ubick. Except for Billy Dee Williams, the father of our classmate Honoko, the parents and guardians of the eighth grade's entire black population were assembled in Mr. Ubick's office. All present agreed that there was a serious problem; I felt gratified when my mother reported back to me that I was not the only one who noticed how Ms. Frischman rendered "black" like it was an off-color word. My mother, however, was the only person willing to file a formal complaint.

Damon's governess and Mark and Brian's parents were afraid that Ms. Frischman would retaliate by failing their kids and preventing them from graduating from middle school. Ironically, because my mother was the only one willing to document her dissent, I became the only student who Mr. Ubick could protect from that very fate.

An arrangement was made where I would show my homework to Mr. Ubick before turning it in to Ms. Frischman. In addition, Ms. Frischman was to notify Mr. Ubick if I ever fell below a "C." Mr. Ubick was particularly sensitive to the race issue because he had a black son-in-law. As he told my mother, he did not care that his daughter had married a black man--in fact, he described his son-in-law as being "exemplary"--however, he was concerned about the impact race would have on the lives of his grandchildren.

As everyone feared, Ms. Frischman did retaliate by giving me an "F" for a final grade, but Mr. Ubick overrode her and changed my grade to a "C." I don't know what happened to Mark and Brian, but I suspect that their 4.0 GPAs insulated them from any of Ms. Frischman's shenanigans. Damon was not so lucky. Ms. Frischman gave him a failing grade, and even though she was fired, Damon was not permitted to graduate.

The last time I saw Damon and Mr. Ubick was at the dance celebrating graduation. Even though Damon was not graduating, he was allowed to attend the party because his family supplied most of the music. In the months preceding graduation, it struck me that my interactions with Damon were becoming particularly contentious, though I could never tell whether he was joking or being serious.

One morning, for instance, Damon accused me of spreading lies about him and offered to settle the matter with another fight. I couldn't get Damon to tell me what type of lies, nor was I able to convince him that I was innocent. The whole day was spent with Damon demanding that I stop telling lies about him and me proclaiming my innocence to no avail. At one point, some of my classmates joined me in a chant that we approached Damon with, "What Lies, what lies?" Finally, at the end of the school day, Damon confessed that it had all been a hoax--he was the one who had been telling lies.

I knew Mr. Ubick liked me because, once or twice, he handed me a granola bar when we passed each other in the halls. So, I wasn't surprised when my mother said that Mr. Ubick told her that I was a wonderful and mature kid. With Damon, I was certain I had made a permanent enemy. So, I was surprised when my mother also told me about a conversation she overheard in which my name came up, and Damon responded by saying how he'd always liked me and was going to miss me.

Chapter Three:
Terrible Teens

R ight before starting at Beverly Hills High School, I took two summer school courses in preparation for the upcoming fall. It was a year's worth of European History in six weeks, and I loved it. Even the likes of Ms. Frischman couldn't dampen my enthusiasm for history, and I was studying a part of the world I was about to visit. My lifelong dream of going to France was about to come true with a two-week stay in Paris at the end of the summer.

The summer school routine was intense: four hours of Early European History in the morning, an hour lunch break, then four hours of Modern European History in the afternoon. I found the ability to focus on one thing both comforting and exciting. Another aspect of my personality emerged as, in the morning class, I became the human encyclopedia everyone consulted before our daily quizzes, and in the afternoon class, I was the expert who knew all the answers and could expound on the previous night's reading assignment during class discussions.

A highlight of the year I spent at Beverly Hills High School was my participation in choir and drama. Despite my tendency towards introversion, there was always a part of me that loved the limelight. One of the things I loved most about participating in choir was the opportunity to perform in public, like the time we sang Christmas Carols at the Beverly Center Mall. My favorite part of drama class was the section on improvisation. The teacher would choose a couple of students and then create a scenario for them to run with and turn into a narrative. I was always happy when it was my turn. My two best friends, Demitri and Benji (both of who I had met in summer school), were somehow able to help me further shed my cloak of introversion; when I was around them, I could be a real comedian.

My favorite academic class was English. I got along famously with the teacher, who, like my mother and me, had vacationed in France, and we would share memories of our experiences there. I was also an excellent student. There was one assignment that I consider pivotal in my development as a writer; we had to write a summary of a chapter in the novel To Kill a Mockingbird in exactly twenty-five words. It forced me to synthesize my ideas while also instilling in me the habit of writing succinctly, something that came in handy when I wanted to write poetry but proved problematic when I needed to expound more fully in prose.

The assignment was similar in form to the seven-sentence paragraph I was introduced to in fifth grade: break whatever you have to say down into a topic sentence, major detail, minor detail, major detail, minor detail, major detail, and a conclusion. My mother objected to this mechanical approach to writing instruction. As she always said, "writing is thinking on paper." I wanted to believe her. I wanted my words to flow on the page as they did in my head. However, it would be years before I could free my mind and internalize my mother's wisdom about writing.

My math class was not much of a math class. We basically spent all our time learning how to write checks and balance checkbooks. The closest we ever came to any real math was during a test of our ability to follow directions. The first item on the test was an instruction to not answer any of the questions until we had read through the entire exam. Many of my classmates failed to heed this instruction and went straight to work attempting to solve the 100 or so algebra and geometry problems, and they were mortified when the teacher called "time" after only about 15 minutes.

The trick, as I and some of my other classmates who followed that first instruction discovered, was that there was no need to complete any of the math problems in order to finish the exam. The last question told us that we only had to answer the first three, which asked for our names and some other basic information.

Our math teacher was very big on following rules, a priority she emphasized by locking the door as soon as the bell rang. She even seemed to think her authority extended to our parents. When my mother suggested that marking students tardy for being a minute late was unreasonable, the teacher fumed, "What? Are you questioning my policy?"

Unlike Hawthorne, Beverly Hills High School didn't have a popular group—at least not one that I could firmly delineate—but Elana was one of the most popular girls in the school. However, she was not stuck-up, and she was a very nice person. She had a very distinctive, high-pitched voice that was as sympathetic and warm as her personality. To me, Elana was a bit of an enigma. I could never figure out how she felt about me. When I asked her to a school dance, she neither said "yes" nor "no" but that she would meet me there. When I sent her a Valentine-o-Gram, she responded by giving me a big hug, but that was pretty much the end of it. At the end of the year, I was pleasantly surprised when Elana wrote in my yearbook, "You're an inspiration to me."

Another girl I liked was Keisha, one of the few black girls in the school, whose voice was as captivating to me as Elana's. In fact, Keisha and Elana were like the black and white versions of each other; both were short, plump, and pretty. Like Elana, Keisha also gave me a big hug when I sent her a Valentine-o-Gram. Unfortunately, a short time later, Keisha disappeared, and I later learned that she had been expelled after being caught drinking alcohol on the school grounds. The last time I spoke with Keisha, she seemed happy to hear from me. She said she was about to go and get her hair done and would call me when she got back. A week passed, and I hadn't heard from Keisha. When I expressed concern about this during a conversation with my grandmother, she suggested humorously that I should be patient; maybe Keisha was still getting her hair done. That was over 30 years ago.

As happy as I was in high school, I was still given to adolescent angst. I felt that I really wasn't connecting with people. My classmates would be friendly, even solicitous, but our interactions seemed to freeze and move no further. Once, when I was feeling particularly alienated and out-of-place at a school dance, I brooded over the nature of my insignificance. I wondered whether it was possible that I was only put on this Earth to serve as a statistic, to maybe add to the body count in some natural or man-made disaster, but beyond that, I was a person of no importance.

Fortunately, my existential pessimism was offset by making the Dean's List. I remember how in my excitement, I naively likened it to being appointed to the President's cabinet, an assertion my mom found particularly galling since I had just emerged from one of my funks. More realistically, my lifelong dream of spending a year in France was about to come true. My mother was writing her dissertation on the two film adaptations of the novel <u>Native Son</u> by Richard Wright, an expatriate writer who had lived in France. Wright's definitive biographer was a Frenchman named Michel Fabre, and my mother was going to Paris to work with him.

While my mom and I were living in France, the movie *Rainman* came out in theaters, and we saw it in English with French subtitles. I enjoyed the film and appreciated the opportunity following both the subtitles and the dialogue gave me to improve my French vocabulary, but beyond that, the film held little significance for me. I was surprised when my mother mentioned that I was autistic during a conversation about the film with a friend of ours. Yes, I remembered the Autism-Residual State diagnosis, but it too made little impression on me except to maybe suggest that whatever was wrong with me, it wasn't autism.

I'd always known I was different, but in France, I discovered that difference was relative; I went to a French public school with several private international sections, so my classmates came from all over the world. In a way, everyone was different. Even what I took to be my unique family situation—being raised by a single mother and having little to no contact with my father--was rivaled by those of some of my classmates.

The American Section was divided into three basic, though unique, personal narratives. There were kids who were the product of Franco-American liaisons; they had been born and raised in France, and their American parent wanted them to retain a bit of American culture. There were kids who were 100% French; they had been born and raised in France but had spent maybe a year or two in the United States, and their parents, too, wanted them to retain a bit of American culture. Then, there were the kids like me who were 100% American, had been born and raised in America, and whose parents were in France on business. And, in France, for the first time in my life, I really was 100% American. I wasn't Afro-American or black American; I was simply American. As far as my classmates and teachers were concerned, I walked, talked, dressed, and even looked like a typical American.

Ironically, my first experience of culture shock came not from the four classes I took in French taught by French teachers but from the two classes, I took in English taught by an American teacher. I don't remember if it was for the American history or literature class, but one of our first assignments was a take-home essay question. I answered the question in a paragraph when the teacher had been expecting several pages. And my classmates seemed to have understood without needing to be told that an essay of some length was required.

An in-class essay question left on the chalkboard from another class gave me a sense that the assumption of length was not just a particular quirk of my American teacher but a schoolwide norm. When I saw the word "developez," (which in this context roughly translated to "expand on that"), I felt a moment of panic for the students confronted with that assignment and a sense of relief when I reminded myself that I was not one of them.

Understanding that I needed to write a lot more, unfortunately, didn't make it any easier to do so. I enjoyed the books we were reading, but I couldn't put things together in a way that would produce an extended argument. It was like I was completely incapable of any kind of critical analysis. Incidentally, an inability to analyze was responsible for why I was in school in the first place. I still marvel at the complete lack of imagination I displayed when I insisted upon going to school when my mom and I moved to France. My mother offered me the option of not going to school, but I just didn't see that as feasible. How was I going to meet people? How was I going to socialize? I am also amazed at my choice of a school in a suburb of Paris over one that was in the heart of the city.

What was the problem with the school in Paris? Most of the classes were taught in English, and I thought I would only become fluent in French if I was completely immersed in the language. That's how my foreign classmates had learned English. At the Lycee International in St. Germain-en-Laye, a suburb of Paris, most of the classes were taught in French.

I don't so much regret my decision (and I appreciate the fact my mom respected me enough to let me make one), as much as I see it highlighting the limited perspective of my younger self. My mom and I had a wonderful time in France, and I loved going to school at the Lycee. My mother and I rented an apartment in Le Ciel St. Cloud, a suburb of St. Germain-en-Laye, so we didn't get into Paris as much as we might have liked (there was a train that connected to metro, but one or both were often on strike), but we did have an opportunity to travel around Europe.

For the sake of convenience, my mother bought a car which came in handy when my grandfather came for a visit. During World War II, my grandfather had been stationed in Alsace-Lorraine, where he drove ammunition and troops to the front lines. One night his truck hit a tree, and he lost his leg. He would wear a prosthetic limb for the rest of his life. When my grandfather came to France, my mother drove him and me to Epinal, the small town where he had been stationed almost a half-century earlier. Being back in Epinal didn't trigger any memories for my grandfather; however, he did enjoy our visit to the War Museum in Caen and being present for the memorial commemorating the 45th anniversary of the storming of Normandy Beach.

The trip to Normandy inspired one of my first spontaneous pieces of creative writing. I wrote a short story in which I imagined the Battle of Normandy from three different perspectives: a soldier storming the beach, a gunner firing from the cliffs on the beach, and an airman flying overhead. The story, itself, was pretty good, but my mother was particularly impressed with the title "A Day at the Beach."

- - -

My mother and I had heard about Loyola High School, a private, Jesuit, college preparatory school in Los Angeles, from a merit badge counselor about a year before we moved to France. Because I was transferring from a French high school, my first year at Loyola was eclectic: included were a ninth-grade history class called "Global Studies" (a required course for all Loyola students), an eleventh-grade French course (taught completely in French), and a tenth grade Bible Studies course called "Pathways Through Scripture." One of my classmates liked to joke with me as we passed each other in the halls between classes "so, what grade are you in this period?"

My French teacher, Mme. Cane was an American woman who was married to a Frenchman. Her French accent was so flawless that the few times she uttered anything in English, it was like a scene from The Exorcist—she spoke with the voice of a completely different person. My "Pathways Through Scripture" teacher was a Priest who had wanted to be a Priest for most of his life. Father Cicone compared himself to some of the figures we were studying in the Bible who needed to be called three times by God before responding. In the case of Father Cicone, his parents kept telling him, starting at age five, to wait before making the decision to become a Priest.

There was one class in which Father Cicone presented us with a paradox that became, for me, a bit of a riddle; he asked, "can an omnipotent God create a rock too heavy for him to lift?" Of course, he can—he's omnipotent, he can create anything, but then there is no object that he cannot lift. Talk about being caught between a rock and a hard place. Years later, I had an epiphany, a realization that God could be said to have created something over which he has little or no control. While taking a cool shower after an invigoratingly hot sauna, the perfect context for feeling inspired, a thought suddenly emerged from my stream of consciousness "free will is the rock God created too heavy for him to lift, and he did it deliberately."

One of the supposed advantages of going to an all-boys school is that girls are not a distraction. I'm still tickled by the naiveté of that presumption. There may not have been any girls in the school, but they were ever-present in our minds. Almost every joke ended with sexual innuendo as a punchline; "have you gotten laid?" was just as much a form of greeting as "what's up?"; and one of my classmates even had racy photos of bikini models affixed to his notebook.

A unique strain of resistance in this male culture, this petri dish of testosterone, was a kid named Robert, easily the smartest person in the school. Robert once dazzled my French class during our final exam by writing eight pages to everyone else's two to three; he impressed the whole school when he appeared on Jeopardy (he also amused us when he misspoke and gave the name of a fellow student as an answer to a question); and he surprised me one day when in response to a rolled-up girly magazine being passed around he declared "that's no way to treat women."

When my classmates at Loyola were not obsessing about sex, they were ruminating about race, or more specifically, my race. I, a lightly tanned recent arrival from France, became the object of a different type of hegemonic gaze. "Where are you from?" "Are you mixed?" "You can't be black." Before this, I never thought that my fair skin had any meaning. In fact, I felt quite dark growing up in Beverly Hills—even darker than some of my olive-skinned Iranian classmates. Through the lens of Loyola, however, the connection between two strange, disparate incidents came clearly into focus.

I remembered the neighborhood kid that wanted me to join him in roasting one of our black playmates by calling him "nigger." At the time, I thought the invitation was an indirect way of calling me "nigger," and being stunned and confused by what seemed like a request for permission to insult another black person in the same way I had just been insulted, the only thing I could think to do was to withhold my endorsement.

Then there was the summer I spent at Camp Atwater, a predominately black camp in Springfield, Massachusetts. As far as my peers were concerned, I was white. I had trouble fitting in at first, but then I became "cool" even though I was white, and when my grandparents visited me from New York, one of my new friends remarked in awe how my brown-skinned grandmother "looked" black.

Was I really that light? Yes, according to my classmates at Loyola. This obsession with my identity seemed to be shared by people outside the walls of Loyola. I couldn't get a haircut without being asked to explain why I had kinky hair. The only explanation I could offer was a history lesson. I had done a genealogy chart in fifth grade, and I had traced my family back to my great-great-grandparents. So, I knew all my relatives on both sides of my family were black going way back to at least to the mid-1800's.

True, my maternal grandmother's grandparents were both half Caucasian; my maternal grandfather's parents were both half Native American; my paternal grandmother was Puerto Rican; and my paternal grandfather and great-grandfather were from Antigua and Venezuela, respectively. But all of them had that "one drop of black blood" that determined race in the United States. So, they were black; it's as simple as that. Besides, a lineage of mixture is not unique to me. It's the story of America, a story I just happen to wear on my face.

Even after giving a version of my family history, I would still get a bad haircut because few people knew how to cut kinky hair regardless of its origins. On the flip side, people who did have experience with kinky hair always wanted to sculpt my hair and give me some fancy style when all I wanted was for my hair to be shortened and trimmed. Because of this, haircutting was added to my mom's list of parenting duties. In the last few years, I've noticed that more people seem to know how to cut my hair. I don't know if it is because I'm older and people react to me differently or if I've just lived long enough to witness some social change.

My adventures in hair cutting must have been shared by one of my mother's black former students who cut his own hair and who my mother recruited to cut mine the day before I had a date. "Who's the lucky girl?" he asked. Feeling lucky myself, I proceeded to recount the story of how I met this girl at a dance a couple of weeks earlier; how we seemed to click immediately, how by the end of the evening I had her phone number, and how after a few phone conversations she agreed to meet me at a local mall. Looking back, I can laugh at my optimism. That date never took place; the girl stood me up—twice.

A date that did take place gave my mother and me another opportunity to indulge in optimism. Through a friend of one of my aunt's, I met teenage actress Kent Masters, one of the few African Americans to star in a Soap Opera. One night, Kent and her mother (my aunt's friend) came to our apartment for a visit. One of my mother's friends was also there. At the end of the evening, the consensus was that Kent seemed interested in me. I asked Kent to a school dance, and she said "yes." My mother drove us and picked us up, and when she saw Kent and me standing outside the school, she said the tableau put her in mind of her standing next to my father.

In truth, I never had a chance with Kent. Not only was she more inclined to date someone closer to her socio-economic status, but also, she preferred older men who she felt were more mature. However, I probably made matters worse by something I did or failed to do on the way to the dance. With my mother in the driver's seat and me in the passenger seat, Kent sat by herself in the back of the car. And, after a perfunctory greeting when my mother and I picked Kent up at her house, I didn't utter a single word, content to just sit in silence and stare out the window. It never even once occurred to me to do otherwise. Indeed, I wasn't even aware of my behavior until my very disappointed mother brought it to my attention later.

The first dance I went to while at Loyola was in collaboration with one of our sister schools, and I made quite an entrance in my beige suede jacket and slacks with a tucked-in collared shirt. Everyone else was dressed in baggie jeans or khakis partially covered by overhanging casual, albeit collared, shirts. I became acclimatized to the teenage dress code almost immediately—learning how to dance was going to take some doing.

Like most teenagers, I loved music and was rarely without my Walkman and headphones. However, I much preferred listening to music than dancing to it. Having no allegiance to any channel, artist, or even particular type of music, I would roll up and down the channels searching for those songs that held personal significance for me. I relished the privacy of my own thoughts as my brain pulsated to the beat; the headphones were crucial to me because I didn't want people to hear what I was listening to, knowing that they would never understand the unique associations being evoked for me by the music. At school dances, I was usually content to just sit and listen to the music. Occasionally, the DJ would play a particularly vibrant song that made me feel compelled to move. At that point, I'd just let loose, and I might get lucky and manage to move my body in socially appealing ways.

My mother taught me how to dance in much the same way that she taught me how to walk, except the former was a lot more fun. There was no excitement to be had in walking across the living room floor carrying small dumbbells in my hands, but I always enjoyed myself when my mother would play music and show me how best to move on the dance floor. Did my mother's lessons take? Well, I no longer waddle like a duck or jerk like a chicken, but I still walk far better than I can dance.

- - -

I can't pinpoint exactly when my life began to spiral into what would eventually culminate in a definitive diagnosis of autism. I would later be told that because of my autism, I experienced (and my mother experienced) exaggerated adolescence. I call it my "Terrible Teens." I always had a bad temper. When I wasn't getting into fights on the playground, I was yelling at my mother in response to what I saw as constant criticism. Most of the criticism was perfectly justified, but I would react to it before I had time to think about it. In many ways, I was a perennial screw-up. When I wasn't putting off homework assignments to the last minute, I was misplacing important documents and losing jackets.

I didn't take criticism any better than I took teasing—in a way, I saw the two as synonymous. It's not that I thought my mother was teasing me; it's just that when I got into a certain state of mind, I saw anything disagreeable as an attack. My automatic response was to raise my voice, and my mother would also raise her voice. I'd start talking faster than I could think, and my defense of myself would become more incoherent as its volume increased. My mother would remind me about the neighbors, which only enraged me more. The next day, of course, while I was taking out the garbage or getting the mail, my own awareness of the neighbors would be magnified as if to make up for the lack of consideration I showed them the night before.

As I entered my mid-teens, my outbursts became more frequent, and I started involving other people. I would call my grandfather in New York and keep him on the phone for hours ranting about everything from my mother's failings to the history of race relations in the United States. My grandfather, struck by the creative way I put things together during some of my ravings, came up with a unique theory about what might be wrong with me.

"Your grandfather thinks you might have a seizure disorder," my mother informed me.

"How would that make me speak brilliantly?" I asked.

"Intense brain activity," my mom explained.

That conversation reminded me of the bit of humor added to a French conjugation lesson, "Elle est sage quand elle dour" ("She is wise when she sleeps"). I didn't get the joke, so I asked my mother to explain it.

"Can you imagine someone who is only wise when they sleep?"

So, there it was, leave it to me to be "sage quand Je suis fou" (wise when I'm mad).

My grandfather's theory was just one of many of the lay explanations for why I was having outbursts. Some of the other theories included the anxiety of living in my mother's intellectual shadow, a bad temper inherited from my father, emotional problems caused by the absence of said father, an identity crisis, black rage, and run-of-the-mill growing pains. The peanut gallery crackled, "Kick him out of the house," "Stop putting so much pressure on him," "Any black man outta be angry," "Sounds like Schizophrenia," "He's just like his father, "It's normal for a teenager to be out of control."

My mother and I considered all these possibilities and more, but she managed to remember that I had once been called autistic, even if only in retrospect. However, when my mother brought this up at one of my first appointments with Dr. Munford, a psychologist at UCLA, he dismissed the notion out-of-hand as being ridiculous. Dr. Munford gave me some psychological tests, the results of which he felt were inconclusive, and concluded that I suffered from Social Phobia.

- - -

The night I was admitted to the hospital, I had written a suicide note decrying "the roller coaster of life" and declaring, "this is where I get off." As I told the admitting nurse, my opinions on the matter of taking my own life were just as unstable as I found life itself. I didn't like this instability, the extremes that my life and my moods seemed to cover. I could go from being hopeful to the point of euphoria to being pessimistic to the point of despair. My anger was the same way. I was either placid, or I was wild. I didn't get angry; I got enraged.

There was a surprisingly humorous side to my interchange with the admitting nurse. It began with a set of questions meant to determine my cognitive awareness.

"How old are you?"

"17."

"What year is it?"

"1991."

"Who is the President of the United States?"

"George Bush."

"Can you name the last five presidents?"

"I think so…Reagan, Carter…Ford, Johnson, Kennedy…"

"You forgot Nixon, but that's a good thing."

Returning to more serious matters, the nurse asked if there was mental illness in my family, to which my mother responded in the affirmative and gave a brief history. While no one in my family had ever been diagnosed with a mental illness, some of my relatives had engaged in behaviors that suggested mental problems. After the intake interview, my mother and I had to wait while the psychiatrist-on-call was paged so that I could be admitted. We waited for hours. It was about 7 pm when my mother and I arrived at the emergency room; by the time I was taken to the adolescent ward, it was after midnight.

At 17, I was the oldest patient in the adolescent psych ward. Everyone wanted to know why I was there, and when I think back on the stock answer I gave, I am amazed at my evasiveness. "You know what they say; the teenage years are the hardest." But, in a way, I was being serious; it seemed to me that part of what I was experiencing was the growing pains that I had been warned about in middle school. There was evidence that I was not alone. A classmate I looked up to once confessed to me that he was confused.

"Confused about what?"

"I don't know. I'm just confused."

The other patients seemed to know exactly why they were there. During group sessions, the one-to-two-word explanations were offered effortlessly as we went around the circle, "eating disorder… family problems…depression…OCD," and they always stayed the same. My answers changed. Sometimes I'd say depression, not comprehending that Depression was a clinical diagnosis. Other times, I'd say family problems, though I tended to stay away from that because I didn't want to blame my mother for my problems. Eventually, I was able to settle on autism.

While Dr. Munford saw my stay in the hospital as an opportunity for respite and a safe way to conquer my social anxieties, I was also in the hospital waiting to be evaluated by Dr. BJ Freeman for a diagnosis of autism. By this time, Autism-Residual State was no longer considered valid. Autism was now seen as a lifelong condition—not something that could become residual--and a determination had to be made as to whether I had the disorder.

Dr. Warren, the psychiatrist in charge of the adolescent ward, felt an intellectual affinity with my mother because she was an English professor. As he put it, my mother and he were both like detectives engaged in analyzing clues in order to solve puzzles. My mother would tell me about conversations she had with Dr. Warren in which they interacted almost like colleagues.

It was Dr. Warren who introduced my mother and me to the concept of Asperger's Syndrome. As fate would have it, my hospitalization coincided with what turned out to be a watershed year in autism history. In 1991, Hans Asperger's 1944 paper on autism was made available in the United States, and even though Asperger's Syndrome would not be officially recognized as a diagnosis until 1994, the condition was already being discussed in the psychiatric and psychological literature. Dr. Warren felt that I would probably classify as having Asperger's Syndrome because of my intelligence and verbal ability.

Dr. Warren also helped exonerate my mother from the parental blame that still, unfortunately, tended to accompany the understanding of autism. Though she was never called a "refrigerator mother," the dubious concept that linked autism to cold, emotionally distant parenting; there was tacit criticism of my mother in the hospital admissions form which listed "parent/child conflict" and a report that stated a social skills group had been recommended for me when I was 11 years old.

Dr. Warren explained that the "parent/child conflict" listed on the admissions form was not a diagnosis or even an explanation but simply a description of what brought me to the hospital. Equally important, when my mother showed Dr. Warren the original 1985 report in which Dr. Freeman advised my mother to just keep doing what she was doing, Dr. Warren got the later report which implied my mother failed to follow medical advice amended to more accurately reflect what really happened.

I was in the hospital for three weeks, and my discharge coincided with mid-term week at Loyola. While my mother and I had been assured that the hospital school would keep me in sync with the high school curriculum at Loyola—even down to receiving homework assignments from my teachers—it turned out that no one at Loyola (except for my academic advisor, whom my mother had informed herself) even knew I had been hospitalized. On the one hand, I was free to give my teachers and my classmates any explanation I wanted for my absence from school. I told everyone I had suffered a major asthma attack. On the other hand, I now had less than a week to catch up on a semester's worth of reading. The pressure got the better of me, I had another outburst, and I wound up being readmitted to the hospital less than two weeks after I had been discharged.

During my second hospitalization, Dr. Warren's rotation ended, and he was replaced by a Dr. Saunders, who came to a very different conclusion about what was wrong with me. In many ways, my second hospitalization was identical to my first. Dr. Munford still felt I needed respite and social desensitization, and I was still waiting to be evaluated by Dr. Freeman for a diagnosis of autism. The major difference was Dr. Saunders' opinion that I was a Paranoid Schizophrenic, an assessment that she felt was bolstered by my very own words regarding my father and my orthodontist.

When my parents divorced when I was 2 years old, my mother was awarded full custody, and my father was required to pay $100 a month worth of child support. My father ignored the court order, and whenever my mother pressed the issue, he claimed to be poverty-stricken. Then, when my father made a hit record in 1986, my mother sued for child support and was awarded retroactive payments as well as $1200 a month until my 18th birthday.

This time my father complied with part of the court order; he willingly paid the back child support and the $1200 a month, but he refused to pay any of my medical bills.

Meanwhile, my orthodontist refused to see me until he was paid, which meant that my braces festered in my mouth for about a year longer than they should have.

When I relayed some of this story to Dr. Saunders, I expressed anger at both my father and my orthodontist. What disturbed me about my orthodontist was that he was always so friendly and chatty. I felt a sense of betrayal from this doctor who, on the surface, seemed so solicitous of my well-being but who showed he couldn't have cared less about me. I don't remember exactly how I put it, but somehow, I managed to convey to Dr. Saunders that I thought my orthodontist was out to get me.

I was prescribed the anti-psychotic drug Haldol to treat my paranoid delusions and Cogentin to offset the side effects of the Haldol, the most prominent being the risk of developing Tardive Dyskinesia aka, a chronic, slow-onset involuntary movement disorder. While the prospect of developing Tardive Dyskinesia was scary enough, Haldol's most disturbing side effect had no offsetting agent. It was like my body and brain were no longer connected. For instance, when I sat down, the downward sensation would continue even after I made contact with the seat, but without the clarity of feeling like I was falling. It was like being stuck in a type of perceptual limbo.

I might have remained in limbo forever if not for Dr. Bernard Rimland, the experimental psychologist who helped establish that autism was a biological condition and not the result of poor parenting. My mother had been a longtime member of the Autism Research Institute, which was founded and directed by Dr. Rimland, and she managed to get the doctor on the phone. Dr. Rimland warned my mother that if she did not get me out of the hospital before my eighteenth birthday, there would be nothing she could do to prevent me from being confined indefinitely. My mother took Dr. Rimland's counsel and "against medical advice," had me discharged from the hospital just days before Dr. Saunders was planning to increase the dosage of Haldol.

Chapter Four: Diagnosis, Autism

"So, why do you want to be autistic?" That's the first question I remember Dr. Kahn, a psychologist with the Westside Regional Center, asking me when I was being evaluated for a definitive diagnosis of infantile autism. "Because it certainly beats just being crazy, lazy, and stupid," I was almost tempted to joke but, fortunately, did not since Dr. Kahn, as I later learned, had decided to take every word I said at face value.

My actual response to the "why-do-you-want-to-be-autistic" question was good enough, and years later, a psychiatrist reading Kahn's final report would tell me that he found my words--"if I get lost, and people don't know I'm autistic, they won't look for me"—moving and powerful. What stands out to me, however, about Kahn's final report are some of the more unfortunate things I said that are forever etched in ink and recorded for posterity. While some of the things I said were certainly alarming, I think they were made worse by the fact that Dr. Kahn took them literally. As far as she was concerned, I couldn't be speaking figuratively or expressing my fears and my resentments using analogy and metaphor; I could only be speaking factually and concretely. After all, autistics are literal thinkers, and I was there to be diagnosed with autism.

During my interview with Dr. Kahn, I made the mistake of free-associating about the darker side of intelligence. I openly speculated about the possible negative effects of trying to grapple with my new identity. In addition to introducing me to my autism, my sojourn in the hospital awakened me to my intelligence. Indeed, intelligence seemed to be an integral part of my autism. Not only did I have the advanced vocabulary associated with my particular brand of autism, but also there was the concept of autistic intelligence, as formulated by Hans Asperger in his paper on autism, which suggested that originality was an inherent part of my personality.

Growing up, I thought little of my intelligence. I knew I had a good memory, but I would never have considered myself smart. I was certainly nothing like my mother, and any mental abilities I might have seemed of little if any use to me. Nor were they of any particular concern or interest. My hospitalizations changed all that. Based partially on the way I spoke, the other patients considered me a genius. Even the doctors and staff members, with their presumably more nuanced assessment of my cognitive abilities, seemed to feel that I had a good brain. Indeed, a doctor once prefaced a word of advice with "a smart guy like you," and a staff member confessed that though she wouldn't want any of my emotional difficulties, she did envy my intellect.

But intelligence does not come with a moral compass. A short time before my interview with Dr. Kahn, I came across the autistic tendencies of some of history's most nefarious monsters. Given that I was still smarting from being so misunderstood and knowing myself to be quite apt at harboring a grudge, I had to wonder if I would finally wind up using my newfound abilities for good or for ill. I made the mistake of telling Dr. Kahn the possibility that I might take my talents in the wrong direction. My honesty was rewarded with a diagnosis of thought disorder to go along with my autism.

In fact, nothing I said had any figurative or symbolic potential. For instance, I told Dr. Kahn about my neologisms, the words I make up to describe people. While years after this conversation, a psychiatrist would describe my private language as poetic, Dr. Kahn could only see pathology.

As upset as Dr. Kahn's final report made me, it did serve the beneficent purpose of officially, definitively, and unequivocally diagnosing me autistic. Because I had been diagnosed with a developmental disability before my 18th birthday, I could now receive support services from the Westside Regional Center. By this time, I was living in my own apartment (right across the street from my mother), and people would come in to help me clean, pay bills, cook, and shop. I also started attending a social skills group for autistics at UCLA.

Through a special program at Santa Monica Community College, I had the adult equivalent of an Individualized Educational Program (IEP). While amassing the missing credits needed for my high school diploma, I also took college-level courses. Since I was good in English, I was able to get into the Scholar's Program, which guaranteed me a slot at UCLA, assuming I maintained a "B" average. Meanwhile, I was also taking pre-algebra and being assessed by the school for a possible learning disability.

My preliminary understanding of autism was that it was a coding/decoding problem that impacted my ability to deal with people and understand the nuances of what was said and what I read. My particular brand of autism came paradoxically with a huge vocabulary. So, in essence, I knew a lot of words but just not how to use them. I also read that autism, as a communication deficit, was the ultimate learning disability since communication is so integral to the learning process.

Around this time, I was learning a lot about the positive (or, at least, the not-so-negative) aspects of learning disabilities. Before enrolling in Santa Monica Community College, I did some homeschooling with a teacher from the Bernice-Carlson Middle School, and this teacher told me about her own struggles with dyslexia while taking pride in the fact that John F. Kennedy was dyslexic. At an independent living center for the learning disabled that I would often go to for social events, there was a particularly powerful and inspirational poster hanging in the lobby. Featuring pictures of Leonardo Da Vinci, Thomas Edison, Albert Einstein, Woodrow Wilson, and Winston Churchill, among others, the question was posed, "What did these people have in common?" The answer: "They had learning differences, not learning disabilities. They managed to use their gifts. Will you learn to use yours?"

The final assessment of my learning disability and my right to have academic accommodations revealed no real surprises except for the finding that while my arithmetical skills were weak, my mathematical reasoning was strong. While this did not bring back memories of the good old days when my mother said I was actually good in math, it did reassure me that I could be smart even in areas where I was not. A major stumbling block for me during my first semester at Santa Monica Community College was the final research paper for the political science class I was taking with the Scholar's Program, a paper for which I required a great deal of assistance from my mother.

The stress of trying to complete the paper by the end of the semester got the better of me, and I had a major outburst which led to the police being called (I don't remember if by my mother or a neighbor). Fearing for her safety as well as my own (the responding officers opined that I wouldn't last a night in jail), my mother encouraged me to take an incomplete in the political science class and a leave-of-absence from Santa Monica College. It was during this leave of absence that, ironically, I began to see myself as a writer; and since I had trouble writing at length, I decided I'd become a poet.

While my mother was helping me complete the paper, I took the subject matter and composed a poem. Around this time, my mother and I had the opportunity to attend a conference in Paris celebrating black American writers who had lived in Europe. It was at this conference that I got to share my poem with Ishmael Reed, a noted black writer who my mother had worked for while she was at UC Berkeley in the early 1970s. Ishmael Reed liked my poem and agreed to publish it, as he would some of my subsequent productions, in his Konch Image magazine.

In addition to encouraging me in my own writing, the conference in Paris also highlighted the transformative potential of the written word. I remember one presentation that made a passing reference to how the source material for many literary works can be traced back to the life experiences of the authors. Around this time, I even started listening to music differently. Sometimes a radio announcer would introduce a song by telling a story about the traumatic incident or circumstance that inspired the creation of the song. Even when no such introduction was given, I found myself taking note of where obvious raw feelings of anger and frustration were being effectively channeled into something more aesthetic.

I had left Santa Monica Community College in mid-December; when I returned towards the end of February, everything was different. One major improvement was that I had a new psychiatrist who, while not knowledgeable about autism, was willing to learn. Dr. Bezdek had discovered, during his own review of the existing autism literature, that Prozac, when administered in high doses, can slow down the running and rushing thoughts that can lead to outbursts and meltdowns. The first thing I noticed, after about a week on the medication, was that I got dressed more quickly in the morning.

In contrast to my first semester at Santa Monica Community College, which ended in despair, my second semester filled me with a sense of hope and optimism. I felt I had a full life. I became active in a club for disabled students called Common Boundaries, for whom I came up with the catchy slogan "You're bound to have something in common with us," and I served as the Vice-President. Many of the people in the club were also my classmates in a class called "Personal and Social Awareness," a continuity that created a type of community. The teacher of "Personal and Social Awareness" was one of the facilitators of the Common Boundaries Club. One weekend we all went on a class/club trip to Idyllwild.

The last time I had been to Idyllwild was for a class trip in the eighth grade a few years before being definitively diagnosed autistic. Being back in Idyllwild a couple of years after the diagnosis gave me an opportunity to reflect on how much my life had changed. During the eighth-grade trip, my relationship with Damon (already tenuous in my view) really began to deteriorate almost to the point of blows. Maybe we were what you might call frenemies. That's the only way I can reconcile the escalating conflict that characterized my encounters with Damon during the last months of middle school and his assertion at the graduation party that he would miss me because he'd always liked me.

But now, I was among people who I knew unequivocally were my friends. Also, since my last trip to Idyllwild, I had been through a cataclysmic personal revolution. Being diagnosed autistic was quite literally the end of the world as I knew it. As much as the diagnosis grounded me in a new understanding of things that had previously left me confused, it also left me a little disoriented. Everything had changed. I felt like I was a completely different person; all previous assumptions I had made about myself were null and void. There was no real correspondence between the two Idyllwild trips—I didn't recognize anything, and I don't even know how close I was to where I had been—but returning to a place I had visited before being diagnosed autistic struck me as a type of bookend, nonetheless.

A particularly close friend I had was a fellow aspiring poet named Audrey, who not only shared that particular interest with me but also provided me with a wealth of social activities. While I was at Santa

Monica Community College, I saw Audrey almost every day, either during the week at Common Boundaries meetings and Personal and Social Awareness class sessions or on the weekends when her mother would take us to movies, restaurants, and other outings with members of Audrey's extended family.

One event I went to with Audrey gave me another opportunity to revisit a place I had been to before being diagnosed autistic. We went to Disneyland to see an open-air live rendition of an extravaganza called Fantasia. The last time I had been to Disneyland was with my Boy Scout troop almost a decade earlier. I had managed to get lost and spent hours wandering around the park. Now I was back at Disneyland, but unlike with Idyllwild, I was able to recognize some of the places I had seen before. Audrey, her mother, and I walked past some of the same rides and concession stands that I had come across repeatedly years before while frantically running around looking for my troop. But now, of course, I was not lost, and, in fact, that night, I made an exciting discovery. I finally found a concrete example of ratiocination.

Ratiocination was a concept my mother brought to me from her study of American literature and the writings of Edgar Allen Poe, the father of the murder mystery genre. Ratiocination had to do with combining the best of logic and creativity. As a process, it involved putting all the pieces together rationally then making an imaginative leap to arrive at a novel conclusion. I loved the plot twists in Poe's short stories "Murders in the Rue Morgue" and "The Purloined Letter."

Poe, himself, took on added significance for me when I learned he liked to climb to the top of mountains and spin himself around in circles. Supposedly, Poe did this, as he put it, "to bring the world together as one," but I knew better—he was doing autistic self-stimming. That night at Disneyland, things came together for me, and I had an "aha" moment while watching the performance of Fantasia.

I thought about all the high-tech special effects that went into creating the make-believe world of Mickey Mouse and his friends and decided this was ratiocination in a nutshell. My mom was impressed and confirmed that I was on the right track by adding that what Disney did was called Imagineering.

Another close friend I had was Peter, who I had met through the Scholar's Program. We were taking a literature class together, and he always struck me as being particularly knowledgeable and intelligent. We became friendly during the intermission of a play we had to see and write about for class. Peter and I saw another play together, which showed me how a symptom of my autism manifested itself in the general population.

The play was called *Kvetch*, and it was my introduction to the concept of Kvetching. The basic format of the play was the normal flow of dialogue punctuated by asides from the characters as they expressed the anxieties and fears that were really besetting them while they tried to put on a brave face. Part of the reasoning behind why I was on Prozac was that at high doses, the medication could stop the flow of obsessive thoughts that could lead to outbursts. Beyond that, I knew myself to be prone to racing thoughts and cloying anxieties. It was nice to see that I was not alone.

Peter was my window into normal. One night, he took me out with a couple of his friends for a "guy's night out." There was no drinking involved, but there was plenty of carousing as we went from one diner to another and just hung out. At one location, Peter and I separated from his two friends and got into a fascinating conversation with a couple of women at an adjoining booth. Looking back, I think one or both women might have been interested in Peter, a fact his two friends seemed to have picked up on, and I might have been a bit of an interloper. Or, at least, that's how it started.

I only remember the conversation vaguely, but somehow it turned to the topic of intelligence and self-confidence. I weighed in with my own ideas based in part on what I was learning in a psychology class and a self-esteem workshop I was taking, and I basically held court. By the time Peter and I left the table, the two women were convinced that I must be a genius.

Peter was a lot taller than me, so in addition to the fact I thought he was one of the smartest kids in the class, I quite literally looked up to him. But it also turned out that he looked up to me, which became particularly apparent when I invited him to my Eagle Scout Ceremony. Peter seemed to be almost as excited as I was as he commended me on my "years of dedication and hard work."

The night I passed my board of review, the event that officially made me an Eagle Scout, a classmate I sometimes had lunch with called to tell me how proud she was of me in response to the upbeat message I had left on her answering machine. A lot of people expressed similar sentiments, and for me, achieving the rank of Eagle Scout was a type of vindication. I could now see myself, like the late-bloomers and underdogs I liked to read about, as finally emerging victorious from my struggles.

But there was also a spiritual aspect to my becoming an Eagle Scout. My final project was the refurbishment of a local church a couple of blocks from where I lived. This particular church just happened to be a Lutheran Church, the denomination of my mother. My father was Catholic, and when my parents got married, my mother was forced to promise any children would be given a Catholic upbringing. The closest she ever came to that was by sending me to Loyola. Religion was never a big part of my life growing up.

Around the time I was diagnosed autistic, the local Lutheran Church was a source of solace and social connectedness. My mother and I became friendly with the pastor, a retired English teacher which gave her something in common with my mother who taught English at UCLA. My mother and I started going to church regularly, and I was confirmed a Lutheran. On the day of my Eagle project, I got assistance from classmates, church members, family, and troop members. The importance of becoming an Eagle Scout wasn't simply that I had made it to the top of the mountain but that I had managed to find my place in a caring community.

As much as I valued community, I also embraced my status as an outsider. Indeed, as a member of Common Boundaries, I saw myself as part of a community of outsiders. I had already been primed to see intrinsic worth in being different. While I was in the hospital, I was particularly impressed with the creativity I saw in some of my fellow patients; one illustrative example was the 11- or 12-year girl who rewrote the story of Jack and the Beanstalk from the Giant's perspective. I began to see a correlation between being different and thinking outside the box. My reasoning was simple, if not simplistic; an abnormal person is not going to approach the world in a normal way. Then there was my mother, who had always encouraged me to challenge conventional ideas, and who once deconstructed the word "abnormal" as simply meaning "not normal." She further added that, in the final analysis, being normal has limited value. The people we admire as a society are special.

I became fascinated with the concept of being an original and even saw it as a way to make up for some of my intellectual lacks. Playing off the film *My Left Foot*, about the disabled artist who manages to paint with the only body part that works, I decided that absent a functioning, logical, left-brain, I could be creative and imaginative with "My Right Brain." My interest in creativity was the source of a major objection I had to the autism diagnosis. Being a literal thinker was simply not an option, and, in fact, creativity helped me overcome certain aspects of my disability.

Creative problem solving enabled me to extricate myself out of the type of scrapes I seemed drawn to like a moth to a flame. For instance, as many times as my mother advised me to get my classmates' phone numbers, I never managed to do so, leaving me with little recourse when I had a question about a homework assignment. And while at Santa Monica Community College, history seemed to be repeating itself when my partner for a joint project for our Drama class failed to show up for a planned meeting, and I had no way of contacting her to find out what had happened. I didn't even know her last name.

But this situation had some significant differences that would prove critical. First, my partner and I were practically neighbors; we lived in the same apartment complex. I also knew that my partner had two roommates, a fact that I realized I could now use to my advantage. In place of my usual powerlessness, I could now move forward proactively. I went to the lobby of her building and looked for any mailboxes that had three names on them. I found two, and the first one I happened to pick turned out to be the right one.

My mother pointed out another time in which I had engaged in creative problem solving, and it was something I did that I didn't even recognize as being at all creative. I was on a Boy Scout camping trip during a heavy rainstorm. Even though I was securely in my tent, the rain was coming down so hard, and the ground underneath me was getting so muddy, I was still getting wet. Eventually, I fled my tent and sought shelter in a local public bathroom. I kept myself warm by using the automatic hand dryer. Once, when I was brooding about being autistic and being seen as a literal thinker, my mom said, "Hey, a literal thinker never would have done what you did on that camping trip."

My sense that I could be creative even if I couldn't be smart was best exemplified in an algebra class I took while at Santa Monica Community College. Math to me was still the sum of all horrors. It would be years before I learned the distinction between arithmetic and mathematics and that the latter actually adds symmetry to the world and can be quite appealing. But the process of mitigating my animosity towards math probably started in Mr. Green's Algebra Class with the teacher's support of my penchant for wordplay.

It all started when Mr. Green talked about the importance of presentation when giving us our first homework assignment. Deciding to take the teacher at his word, I turned in my first homework assignment with the following math poem as the cover page:

"A" Math Student

Placing a value
on all prime and composite numbers
I calculate
carefully using exponents, divisibility tests, grouping symbols, and prime factorizations
to simplify
and find LCM's and GCF's.
When dealing with division or subtraction,
I avoid
associating,
commuting, and
distributing.

Subsequently, I created my own publication called "Mathweak Magazine," in which I would list a series of headlines having to do with math. For instance, one headline read "The Calculator You Can't Count On: Math Genius Caught Skimming Money off the Top." It was during the presidential election of 1992 which gave me a lot of material. Two scoops I reported on were "Bill Clinton admits to having once used a calculator but denies having turned it on" and "Dan Quayle stresses the importance of place values in debate with Al Gore."

I shared my "Mathweaks" with a disability counselor who introduced me to a new word, "eclectic." After asking me if I had ever read Oscar Wilde, she said, "you have a beautifully eclectic mind just like him." I wasn't quite sure what "eclectic" meant, but I liked how it sounded. The phrase "beautifully eclectic mind" would become enshrined as a self-stim. When I looked up the word later that evening and discovered it meant "pulling from many different sources," I was pleased and decided that is how I wanted to be.

While at Santa Monica Community College, I took some creative writing courses that revealed some very interesting things about my writing. My teachers tended to feel that I had talent, but there were two things I needed to bear in mind; a poem doesn't always have to rhyme, and when writing a short story, the less exposition employed, the better as codified in the creative writing adage "Show, don't tell." I found this last piece of advice particularly difficult to internalize because I would get lost in my love of language. I understood that normal human conversation was not filled with rhetorical flourishes, but I found them hard to resist, nonetheless.

Santa Monica Community College also marked my introduction to the field of psychology. In a way, my brain had been the subject of scientific inquiry since infancy, and my own experiences with psychologists and psychiatrists made me particularly interested in mental health.

One of the issues addressed in my psych 101 class was the controversy surrounding IQ testing. The teacher gave the class a version of an IQ test written from a black cultural perspective. What intrigued me most about the test was how much the nature of the test determined the correct answer. For instance, one of the multiple-choice questions required choosing the correct definition of the word "Oreo," and two of the descriptions given were "an Uncle Tom" and "a cookie."

Knowing the test was coming from a black cultural perspective, I chose "an Uncle Tom" as the definition of "Oreo," which was the right answer. However, if the question had appeared on a standard IQ test, "a cookie" would have been the more appropriate answer. As an acquaintance pointed out when I related this anecdote years later, both answers were correct.

Another psychology course I took was Interpersonal Communication, a class that gave me some insights into autism even though autism never came up. The course focused on the many barriers that prevent people from truly understanding each other. The major insight from the course was that as basic as communication is to the functioning of human society, it is far from being straightforward or automatic. Any number of psychological factors (from erroneous assumptions to a defensive mindset) can interfere with the clear passage of messages between people. I was fascinated with the fact that miscommunication was not something that I, alone, had to cope with as an autistic, but rather a phenomenon I experienced along with the rest of the human population. It was the mainstreaming of misunderstanding.

During my last semester at Santa Monica College, I completed a project for my drama class that revealed a possible talent in directing, something my mother alluded to with pride some 25 years later. The class, broken up into groups of two, had performed what is called elastic scenes in which the same script was used in different scenarios. The dialogue in the script was deceptively simple, having to do with one person asking another what they did the night before; but the situations generated by the individual dyads were breathtakingly diverse, from a pick-up scene in a bar to two spies passing messages on a park bench, to an obscene phone call, and so on.

I decided, for a final project, to combine all the scenes together into one mini-play in which I had my protagonist go through each of the scenarios from being hit-on in a bar, being mistaken for a spy, to receiving an obscene phone call, and so on. A few classmates agreed to star in my little play, and I had a great time rehearsing with them. The final product was well-received; the teacher told me I had a great eye for scenery, a compliment that took me right back to the disability counselor who compared me to Oscar Wilde, whose plays I'd recently read showed a gift for set design.

Chapter Five:
A College Try

In 1992, my mother received her Ph.D. in English from UCLA, and she was hired the next year as an Assistant Professor at Macalester College in St. Paul, MN. In February of 1993, I accompanied my mother to St. Paul for her on-campus interview, and I fell in love with the place. One of the things I found most intriguing about Minnesota was the thing that would have driven most people away, and that was the weather. Growing up in Southern California, I had no concept of the changing of seasons, and snow was something I only experienced when I went skiing at my maternal grandfather's timeshare in Lake Tahoe. As such, I associated snow with pleasure and play; I had a "Winter Wonderland" view of snow. The idea that snow was something you had to confront in your everyday life was completely new to me.

My first view of snow in the city was filtered through these rose-colored glasses. As cold as it was, I was drawn to this alien landscape that was like one huge ski resort. Even the brownish tire tracks left by passing cars triggered a pleasant association. The canvass reminded me of some creamy sweet I had seen advertised on TV once but couldn't quite place. It would be a couple of years before I realized I was thinking of Cappuccino.

I was also pleased to find that St. Paul was not the backward town I had been expecting. My mother's future colleagues introduced us to a city that was indeed small but in no way small-minded. We were taken to plays and nice restaurants, and we were given a tour of what proved to be a beautiful campus. I was particularly interested in Macalester's creative writing program. When I learned that the campus bookstore was called The Hungry Mind, I was sold.

My mother was offered the job, and she took it. If I applied to Macalester and was accepted, 90% of my tuition would be paid. Based on my grades and the fact that I was in the Scholar's Program and the Alpha Gamma Sigma Honor's Society, I was told that the chances of me getting into Macalester were good. In my personal essay, I spoke openly about my autism and framed my diagnosis as a learning experience.

I was rejected from Macalester and advised to apply to one of the sister schools in the Twin Cities area. When my mother and I met with the Dean of Admissions to find out why I had been rejected, he said he had made a mistake, and he apologized for what he called "a miscarriage of justice." I still wonder if the mistake he was referring to was relying on the image of autism he had in his mind before seeing me in person. To rectify the situation, I would go to one of Macalester's sister schools while taking a couple of courses at Macalester with a guarantee of being admitted the following year.

I applied to Augsburg College and Hamline University, two institutions in the same consortium of colleges and universities in the Minneapolis/St. Paul area and I was admitted to both. I finally chose Hamline based in part on their glossy brochures and catalog but mainly because of location: Augsburg was in Minneapolis, and both Hamline and Macalester were in St. Paul. Since I would be taking classes at Macalester and Hamline was practically next door to Macalester, Hamline was geographically (and academically according to one of my mother's new colleagues) the better choice.

One of my first experiences of culture shock had nothing to do with the weather or being new to Minnesota. It had to do with my introduction to the new normal in mental health care where psychiatrists no longer administer therapy but instead only see patients for medication management. Counseling is handled by psychologists, social workers, or psychiatric nurses. In my case, I saw a psychiatrist in private practice a few blocks away from Hamline and a counselor at the University's Health Services.

My psychiatrist, Dr. Humenansky, did not have any experience with autism or Asperger's Syndrome, but she agreed to continue me on Prozac as prescribed by Dr. Bezdek. When my mother and I met with Dr. Humenansky for the first time, the doctor's initial impression of me was that I was a genius, and she immediately suggested that I join Mensa. My mother pointed out that while my language skills were of a high caliber, my weakness in math would prevent me from being able to pass the entrance exam.

My verbal ability led to a bizarre relationship with my first and only college roommate. Even though Macalester supplied my mother with a two-bedroom apartment near the campus (though not rent-free), and I could have lived with her, I opted to live in the dorm so that I could have the whole college experience. My roommate was a foreign exchange student from Russia named Oleg, whose host family lived in the small town of Stillwater, Minnesota.

Oleg and I got along well enough at first. We both had an interest in psychology, and we'd often discuss current events. Having decided that I was a genius, Oleg loved to pick my brain—I once even helped him brainstorm an idea for a paper. Unfortunately, Oleg did not own a computer, and he always wanted to use mine. He also started to complain that my alarm clock was too loud. The conflict that ensued wasn't serious, but it highlighted my difficulties with assertiveness. In short, I had a tendency (still do to a certain extent) to let people take advantage of me. With a letter from Dr. Humenansky, I was granted a medical single room which I would keep for the duration of my college career.

For weekly therapy, I saw a counselor at Hamline's Heath Services named Maryann. One of the major things we discussed was my budding relationship with a senior who lived on my floor named Becky. Becky was a quintessential Midwesterner. She hailed from a small Minnesota town, and her family had been in the state for generations. She had never flown on an airplane, and as far as she was concerned, California was a foreign country. Yet, despite our differing backgrounds (and the fact that she was white, and I was black), Becky and I connected almost immediately. We both were the products of divorce. We both had struggled in school. And we both shared a pride in being iconoclasts. We'd spend hours hanging out in her room (she had a single) talking about anything and everything.

Becky and I first met when she, as a new student orientation leader, helped me move some of my stuff into my dorm room. Ironically, that first encounter almost rendered me the least eligible of mates. My mother had just finished making my bed when Becky and I entered the room with a large duffle bag. While my mother was simply trying to secure me the bottom bunk before my roommate arrived, Becky was struck by what she interpreted as the tableau of a Momma's Boy. "He can't even make his own bed?" To add to the irony, after Becky and I started dating a few months later, she would often do motherly things for me like making me soup when I was up late working on a paper and, yes, even making my bed when she'd spend the night in my room.

Academically, my time was split between Hamline and Macalester with a first-year writing class and an abnormal psychology class at the former, and an introductory communications studies class and a philosophy class at the latter. The philosophy course foreshadowed some of my future thinking about autism. The course itself wasn't that interesting or even informative. Most of the class sessions were spent with the teacher and the students pontificating. There was one significant lecture in which the class was introduced to the philosopher Ludwig Wittgenstein and his concept of fuzzy categories. The designation of something as a game was given as a prime example of fuzzy categories. There are no universal attributes that the various activities called games have in common. Some are played on fields while others are played on boards; some are serious business while others are just for fun; and the heterogeneity of all that we might consider a game goes on.

About ten years later, Wittgenstein's concept of fuzzy categories would take on added significance for me when the philosopher's posthumous diagnosis of Asperger's Syndrome coincided with the controversy over whether high-functioning autism and Asperger's Syndrome were two distinct conditions or just different ways of expressing the same phenomenon. Wittgenstein himself might have conceptualized the problem as an example of fuzzy categories.

The most intriguing insight from the philosophy class came from my mother. My mother's field was English literature, and she specialized in African American literature and film. While I was in the philosophy class, she shared with me some literary criticism documenting how Enlightenment philosophers disparaged the humanity of blacks and defended the institution of slavery based on the latter's inferiority. According to one literary scholar, the slave narrative was part of the black response to this blanket condemnation by the 18th-century intellectual establishment.

As an African American and autistic, it was, perhaps, inevitable that I would see parallels between the two conditions—particularly the link between the slave narrative and the autistic narrative. The assertions experts were making about autistics were, for me, reminiscent of the claims made about blacks during the Enlightenment. Both groups were deemed incapable of higher thought, and complex emotion and both groups fought back by telling their stories.

As much as I could recognize myself in the stories told by my autistic cohorts, there were areas in which I found it difficult to identify. Indeed, I was not good at math, and I didn't have any particular interest in science. And, while many autistic writers seemed to accept even embrace the notion that they were literal thinkers, I found this widely accepted view personally demeaning. I also couldn't identify with the ubiquitous descriptions of sensory issues. Loud noises did not cause me physical pain, I was not bothered by the buzzing of fluorescent lights, and I actually enjoyed giving and receiving hugs.

However, if I really thought about it, I realized I did have a unique set of sensory experiences of my own. Sometimes the combination of a rain-soaked sidewalk and litter physically disgusted me and made me feel contaminated. My repulsion has decreased in the last few years thanks to growing awareness. One rainy day, I realized, to my great relief, that the gross mound in the middle of my path was simply uneven pavement being distorted by water.

I've always had an exaggerated startle response which has decreased with age though some loud noises can still cause me consternation. In order to think more rationally about a sound, I'll muffle it by sticking a finger in my ear. I try to be as inconspicuous as possible so that anyone watching me thinks that I simply have an ear itch. And, though I eat everything, I cannot stand the texture or smell of soft-boiled eggs.

In fact, many of my most acute sensory experiences come to me, courtesy of my nose. The way I see it, I rely on my sense of smell when my vision is not up to the task. For instance, I accept that my hands are clean only after the smell of soap replaces the smell of whatever I'm trying to get off them. I am reassured by the smells of chlorine and bleach (which could be a vestige of my childhood love of swimming pools), and since learning that in some cultures, lemons are used as an antiseptic, I am less concerned about the smell of lemon juice on my fingers—though I still can't stand the stickiness.

But I still couldn't identify with the apparent academic prowess of other high-functioning autistics. It was almost like the high-functioning autistic was your classic nerd—good in academics but bad in sports and socialization. This was not my experience. My struggles in school were far more pervasive, and, in fact, during my first semester at Hamline, I was falling behind in the reading and blocking when it came to writing papers of more than a few pages. I also had trouble staying awake in class even after getting a good night's sleep.

Because two of Prozac's side effects can include drowsiness and erectile dysfunction, and I was having sleeping problems and was in a romantic relationship, Dr. Humanansky reduced my Prozac dosage in half. When I explained part of what was going on, my professors understood; one even shared with me the fact that he had also once taken an antidepressant. During my second semester, in which I took all my classes at Hamline so that I didn't have to deal with the commute, I had official academic accommodations. Each of my teachers was sent a letter from the counseling office stating my need for extra time on papers and exams as well as a note-taker.

Another major accommodation was the ability to take a class pass/not pass, which I opted to do for Biology. Even though I had done well in my 4th and 5th-grade science classes, I still felt that science was a relative weakness of mine. I saw myself as more inclined towards the arts and humanities—anything technical or having to do with the "hard" sciences was quite simply beyond my mastery or interest. But during my second semester at Hamline, I found myself increasingly drawn to the subject matter of my biology class.

The class met in the morning right after breakfast, and, often, as I took a bite of food, I'd find myself imagining the process of digestion. The teacher further brought the subject matter to life by taking the class on a field trip to the University of Minnesota's Medical School. While there, I had an opportunity to watch the beating heart of a dog under anesthesia and to see the open chest cavity of a cadaver; the contrast between living and dead tissue made quite an impression on me. But the highlight of the class was my introduction to brainwave analysis with an electroencephalogram (EEG).

The class was divided into groups of four, and each group recruited volunteers to be hooked up to an EEG while looking at pictures and hearing a paragraph read out loud. The object was to compare the brainwave patterns produced by looking at evocative images versus listening to an emotional passage. By this time, I was certain that I wanted to be a psychologist. I enjoyed the biology class so much and found myself so engaged with the material that I briefly considered going to medical school and becoming a psychiatrist.

I also considered not transferring to Macalester and continuing my education at Hamline. I was all set with my class schedule for the fall, and I was going to be a new student orientation leader like Becky had been when I first met her. But then everything changed. My relationship with Becky collapsed; we had been having problems for months, and things came to a boil that summer. It all started with Becky's compulsion to pick pimples off my face—sometimes squeezing until they oozed puss. My therapist felt that Becky might need a therapist, a suggestion the latter dismissed as a non-starter when I brought it up. Things only got worse as I started having long conversations with my mom about all the problems I was having with the relationship—instead of resolving anything, this only made Becky resent the relationship I had with my mother.

Things escalated when Becky cheated on me with Guy. Guy was a fellow classmate Becky, and I often hung out with, who, it turned out, had been interested in Becky for as long as I had been. As far as Becky was concerned, I had already left her when I chose my mom over her. How had I done this? One night, my mom and I had a fight about Becky, which I turned into an outburst. In response, my mom thought it best that I take some time off from Becky, and I agreed. Becky felt abandoned, and Guy took my absence as an opportunity to make his move, or maybe Becky made the first move. Either way, the two became a couple--as another classmate put it, Guy got Becky on the rebound.

Certainly, I could have remained at Hamline even after my break-up with Becky, but I had already made the decision to transfer to Macalester (another thing Becky held against me because, like many Hamline students, she did not like Macalester) when Hamline notified me that they could not financially or administratively support a Student Affairs Fellowship I had earned. Macalester was perfectly ready, willing, and able to support my Fellowship. So, Dr. Humansky raised my Prozac back to the dosage proscribed by Dr. Bezdek, and as if heeding the call of destiny, I transferred to Macalester like originally planned.

Chapter Six:
My Mother's Apprentice

My mother had long regretted the fact that she was not allowed to home school me. Just from the hours she spent helping me with my schoolwork, she knew she could do a far better job of educating me than my teachers were doing. Since at least the fifth grade, my teachers claimed that they were preparing us for college. However, as a graduate student at UCLA, my mother was teaching on the college level and could attest to the fact that whatever my teachers thought they were doing was not working. Many of my mother's students were the product of the Beverly Hills school system, and she found their level of preparedness severely lacking.

My mother did what she could to supplement my education. Every summer, I was enrolled in my local library's summer reading program, for which my mother would have me read books by and about African Americans. We watched Jeopardy every night, and my mother made critical thinking (whether about current events, popular culture, or even interpersonal relationships) an organic part of my life growing up.

My mother's long-deferred dream of being my actual teacher finally came true when I took a winter term film course with her while I was still at Hamline. When I transferred to Macalester and chose English as one of my majors, my mother's wish would be granted several more times. For my part, I discovered that I could learn as much about life from my mother as one of her students as I did as her son.

The topics covered in my mother's courses were more than just academic theories to be left in the classroom. For me, they were transformative concepts that changed the way I saw the world. One concept that I found particularly relevant to my life was the concept of both/and vs. either/or.

As applied to African American literature, particularly that written by black women, both/and has to do with the rejection of rigid either/or categories that all too often manifest themselves as derogatory stereotypes. In the broadest sense, embracing both/and means recognizing the complexity of life and the nuance of circumstance, that things are not either all good or all bad, that black and white thinking should always be tempered by shades of gray.

I applied the concept of both/and to my autism. Embracing both/and enabled me to come to terms with some of my own contradictions. How can I both have a communication disorder and a way with words? How can I both be an intelligent person and have difficulty in school? Or how can I both care about other people and tend to be self-absorbed?

Autistics are, in essence, accused of failing to embrace both/and in the observation made by some experts that we tend to think in all-or-nothing terms. While I reject this notion on principle as a reductive stereotype, I must admit that when I get into a certain state of mind, I cannot appreciate nuances—things are either this way or that way, and any suggestion to the contrary just leaves me feeling angry and confused.

I found further confirmation for my sense that both/and was a concept to live by in a quote from F. Scott Fitzgerald, who declared "the ability to entertain contradictory ideas while retaining the ability to function is the sign of a first-rate intelligence." Given my propensity to lose my ability to reason when things don't fit neatly into my pre-ordained boxes, I can personally attest to the truth of Fitzgerald's words.

I was particularly pleased to find the concept of both/and affirmed in other classes I took that had nothing to do with literature. For instance, in a physics course, I took for non-majors (with the rather pleasing moniker "physics for poets"), I learned that one of the major advances in the history of physics was the discovery of the photon and the concomitant understanding that light can act as both a particle and a wave.

Another concept I derived from one of my mother's courses was the unique vision of the outsider. One of my favorite characters was Sula from Toni Morrison's novel of the same name, an inveterate iconoclast and social outcast who is best described as "an artist without an art form." There may have even been a bit of autism in Sula for like one of Hans Asperger's patients who deliberately elicited anger because he liked the facial expression, Sula might ask someone an off-the-wall question "not because she was interested in the answer but simply to see [their] face change rapidly (119)." The most surprising impact the writings of Toni Morrison and other African American women authors had on me was in helping me to formulate a concept of masculinity. The male heroes in the novels I read in my mother's classes were not the usual alpha males who achieved dominance through physical strength and prowess. Instead, they commanded respect with their good looks and subtle charisma. One character, Ajax, the male hero in Sula, was even close to his mother.

Like many students at Macalester, I had a double-major; and my second major was Psychology. One of the courses I took as a Psychology major turned out to be a nice complement to the literature courses I was taking as an English major. The course was called

Gender Issues in Mental Health, and the teacher was Janie Strauss, a popular professor whose salt-n-pepper, short-cropped straight hair and slightly lined face marked her as a woman in her late sixties but whose spritely manner and enthusiasm-infused voice left the impression of a very youthful person. One of the books we read in the course was <u>Trauma and Recovery</u> by Judith Herman, a Harvard psychiatrist and expert in Post-Traumatic Stress Disorder (PTSD).

The focus of the book was on the psychological effects of crimes against women like domestic violence and rape. As a teaching tool, the book very succinctly outlined the symptoms of PTSD. While I was reading the book, I was also reading the novels of Toni Morrison for a Toni Morrison Seminar. To my complete surprise, I began to see the characters in the novels exhibiting some of the same symptoms described by Dr. Herman in her book. I shared one particularly vivid description of a character's thought process with my psychology class, and Professor Strauss agreed that I was on to something.

I also shared some of Herman's descriptions of PTSD with my mother, the professor of the Toni Morrison Seminar, and she, too, felt that I was on to something. What resulted was the type of intellectual synergy that was becoming increasingly important to me. Both professors allowed me to submit as a final project a paper on PTSD in Toni Morrison's fiction examining the author's rendering of the traumatic effects of slavery and racism.

This intellectual synergy, or continuity of thought as I liked to call it at the time, carried over to the topic of my honor's thesis, which, incidentally, stemmed from the achievement of another lifelong dream of mine—the opportunity to visit Africa. Like many African Americans, I was always curious about my African heritage, but having a name that came from the Akan language of Ghana made me particularly interested in that country. As fate would have it, my junior and senior year coincided with a study abroad trip opportunity to Ghana thanks to the University of Minnesota' SPAN (Student

Project for Amity Among Nations) Program. The importance of my junior and senior year had to do with the structure of the program; a year spent taking classes and learning about the country followed by six weeks during the summer living with a host family in the country and then a year debriefing stateside that would culminate in a final paper about what I learned.

The SPAN Program had been running strong since its inception at the end of World War II with such distinguished alumni as Walter Mondale and Saul Bellows. Every year a different country was chosen, and it just so happened that the country for the '95-96 year was Ghana. And the write-up of my trip became my honor's thesis: gender roles in a matrilineal society.

A matrilineal society, as I would come to learn, is not the same thing as a matriarchal society; while the latter does denote female hegemony, the former has to do with inheritance through the mother's side of the family. Being raised by my mother, I was always intrigued by what I thought was the women-centered nature of a matrilineal society like the Akan of Ghana. However, even after I discovered that a matrilineal society is still very much patriarchal, I still felt a certain degree of kinship since I have certainly received more from my mother's side of the family in the form of love and support from grandparents and aunts than from my father's side.

While I was in Ghana, I stayed with a family called Moses in Cape Coast. George Moses was a medium-built slender man about my height (5'7') with close-cropped kinky hair and almost ebony dark skin. His wife, Vida, was a heavy-set woman who wore her hair in a bun and shared the same dark skin tone as George; however, she towered over him in terms of height. George and Vida had been together since the late 1970s and were happily married with two young kids.

The house the Moses lived in was a light-colored cement structure that would have fit in perfectly in any beach-front or tropical setting. There were two floors, each with a balcony that lent the sense of openness and airiness to the whole décor. The neighborhood surrounding the house was rustic and rural, palm trees, dirt roads, and patches of grass demarcating different properties. The Moses main apartment was on the ground floor, as was the apartment of another family with whom they shared a telephone.

The second floor belonged completely to the Moses and served as a guest house. That is where I stayed. My lodgings came fully equipped with a master bedroom, living room, bathroom, and dining room. And despite what I had been warned to expect before arriving in Ghana, there was indoor plumbing though there was no hot water. Another surprise was a clue to a possible alternative history of African American culture.

Every New Year's Eve, as per tradition, my mother and I had pig's feet, collard greens, and black-eyed peas. I grew up believing that the origins of this dish went back to slavery when my ancestors were given the discards and had to cook them all day just to make them palatable. However, while my mother and I were staying in the Moses' guest house (my mother had accompanied me to Africa and stayed for a couple of weeks just to get me settled), Vida served us a dinner that included pig's feet. Was this a coincidence?

What if it was a matter of perspective? Here's what could have happened. The leniency some plantation owners offered their slaves during the holiday season included a choice of food. Newly enslaved Africans opted for something that reminded them of home, something that from the master's point of view was a discard. This exchange repeated itself over many generations, except the original context got lost in translation. So, what was originally the slave choosing food that the master considered garbage became the slave being given the master's garbage.

George was an engineering student who was off for the summer, so he had time to take me around to interview different people regarding my research on gender roles. Most of my informants were men about George's age (35) who told me about their married lives so that I could get a sense of how men and women interacted in a matrilineal society. Though I did take it upon myself to interview Vida and Mrs. Blankson, a neighbor the Moses were friendly with, I felt comfortable letting George choose my subjects because I saw it as a clue. Why, for instance, did he only take me to see men?

However, I once had a conversation with George that made me realize that I was making an erroneous assumption about the meaning of gender roles. We were sitting down to a lunch that Vida had just prepared for us, and I thought I'd put a lofty spin on what too often is dismissed as women's work. I declared that the meal just set before us was a work of art, that cooking was an art form. George was way ahead of me. He said, "yes, and cooking is also a science."

Considering that George was studying to be an engineer, could there be any further sign of respect than the fact that he likened what Vida did to a science? I realized I was making certain assumptions based on my Western view of things. I came to recognize that equality and fairness for women were far more complicated than the simple demarcation of who does what around the house.

Back in the United States, the advisor for my honor's thesis was Jack Rossman, the chair of the Psychology Department. I had worked with Professor Rossman before. He was my psych major advisor, and he had directed me on an independent project during the Winter break of my first year at Macalester. Professor Rossman was a Macalester institution. He had been teaching at the college for decades and had even once served as provost. About 6 ft. tall, slender, with short dirty blond hair and glasses, Jack Rossman, looked like a professor. He also had a striking resemblance to the first President Bush. In fact, I once overheard someone confess that when they first saw Professor Rossman during an event in the college chapel, they thought he was the former president and wondered about the absence of the secret service.

The independent project I worked on with Professor Rossman led to my first presentation at an academic conference, a conference, incidentally, organized by my mother. By happenstance, I came across an anthology in the campus bookstore called Black Psychology, and as I thumbed through the book, I heard echoes from my childhood of my mother's concerns about the euro-centric nature of my school curriculum. The issue of race was very much a part of the national discourse. Not only was it during the OJ Simpson murder trial, but also the recently published books The Bell Curve and The End of Racism were big news. And my mother was not the only person concerned about diversity (or the lack thereof). In a course I was taking called Clinical Counseling, a major issue was how to ensure that a therapist was able to work with people from a variety of cultural backgrounds, and Macalester College was in the process of considering instituting a Multicultural Studies Program.

As one of the few faculty of color at Macalester, my mother was inevitably called upon to participate in the debates regarding the structuring and administering of this program from what it should be called (multicultural, ethnic, or something else altogether) to what it should include (only people of color, all marginalized groups, etc.) My mother had always told me about the discussions she had about "Multiculturalism" at Berkeley back in the seventies when Ishmael Reed, one of her professors, coined the term. She invited him to speak at Macalester College. Ishmael Reed had always been an inspiration to me as well as a benefactor like when he published my poetry right after my leave of absence from Santa Monica Community College.

For his part, during his stay in St. Paul, Ishmael Reed shared with me how my relationship with my mother was an inspiration to him. He told me about how his mother, while trying to make ends meet as a black woman in the forties, always managed to look out for him. In looking out for me, my mother spotted an opportunity; she encouraged me to take the <u>Black Psychology</u> anthology and make it a part of my psychology major. Perhaps because of the tenure of the times or because as much of an institution as Professor Rossman was, he still managed to keep an open mind; I was allowed to spend a winter term studying the anthology and writing a paper on it. That spring, I took a writing workshop offered by the English department for people working on long-term projects. The major project I was working on was my honor's thesis on the Matrilineal Akan of Ghana. However, the paper I had written with Professor Rossman in January had been accepted for a panel presentation at the African American Studies Conference to be held at Macalester College in April. While working on my honor's thesis, I was also working on turning my Black Psychology paper into my first major public presentation.

The conference, called "African American Women: Then and Now," was the brainchild of my mother, and it was an interdisciplinary extravaganza. The field of African American Studies was considered from all angles, from literature to history and psychology to popular culture. The participants included noted scholars in various fields as well as undergraduate and graduate students just getting their start in academia. For me, the conference was an affirmation of the life of the mind. Three days of listening to panel presentations and participating in informal discussions all while dining and hanging out with the same group of intellectually curious people was an intensely enjoyable experience. I likened it to being on a retreat.

I sometimes wonder if, after a certain age, the range of what is considered normal becomes wider. When you enter college and, no longer travel in packs with your peers as you attend the same classes simultaneously with the same teachers, there is more room for individual differences. Indeed, a normal college student is pretty much anyone in college regardless of major, class schedule, living arrangement, extra-curricular activities, etc.

In my case, I also benefited from the fact that my mother was a very popular professor. Despite my tendency to be reserved and introverted (a trait that a student who was particularly close to my mother even brought to her attention), I managed to have a standing lunch date with a group of my mother's former students at least twice a week. I didn't mind eating in the campus cafeteria alone; in fact, I often found it quite relaxing. However, I always wanted to be aware of what opportunities for socialization were out there. Whenever I entered the cafeteria, I always did a quick scan to see who was already there. Assuming I didn't see anyone I knew or felt like eating with, I would find a seat located toward the back with a direct view of the entrance but off to the side so that I could surreptitiously scan the entire room by simply looking up from my tray.

I also felt a sense of belonging and camaraderie with other classmates that had never taken a course with my mother. These were people I met in my psychology classes. There was a group of us, all seniors, who spent our last year together with Janie Strauss taking her Gender Issues in Mental Health course in the Fall and then her Clinical Counseling course in the Spring. Like most professors at Macalester, Professor Strauss preferred to run her classes as a discussion in which we would talk about the reading. I'd look forward to these classes as though I were attending a book club meeting.

I also had good one-on-one relationships with my professors. Professor Rossman was as much of an introvert as me, and he rarely showed any emotion. But he once offhandedly mentioned to my mother that he considered us friends. Then there was Janet Schank, the Associate Director of the Counseling Center, who was my de facto mentor. She was also perhaps one of my most ardent cheerleaders.

We never had a formal relationship, but we would often meet for lunch at a nearby café or in her office for informal talks. She introduced me to the work of neurologist Oliver Sacks and his portraits of autistics like animal scientist Temple Grandin and artist Stephen

Wiltshire. Janet Schank had a unique way of conceptualizing my talents that amounted to a cautionary tale. Her refrain was that I had a facility with ideas; I had a way of synthesizing information in intellectually creative ways. But she would also wonder whether I'd become bored with some of my ideas and fail to recognize their significance because they now struck me as commonplace. I sometimes teased that she was actually complimenting me for lacking a Theory of Mind, that quality of being able to see other perspectives considered deficient in people with autism.

All kidding aside, though, some of the experts' pronouncements about autism really grated on me. I couldn't stand the idea that I couldn't stand to be touched, and I felt personally insulted, as I mentioned earlier, by the notion that I was a literal thinker lacking in empathy. My mother suggested that as a psychology major, I had an opportunity to confront these issues head-on. For an independent project, I conducted a study to test the validity of the diagnostic criteria for autism. I distributed a survey to two sets of people—autistics and people who work with autistics—asking the former to what extent they agreed with statements like "I cannot stand to be touched" and the latter to what extent they thought their charges would agree with such statements.

Short of the definitive refutation I'd hoped for of what I considered autism stereotypes, I discovered a spectrum of responses from both my autistic and non-autistic informants. Some autistics did respond to my questions literally and expressed disdain for touch and loud noises. But, as a group, they were not monolithic. There was a range of responses that reflected the diversity and complexity of the condition. And, what I found particularly heartening, my non-autistic informants did not answer the questions based on some abstract concept of autism but instead on the individual characteristics of the autistic they were taking care of, something they made clear in the marginalia and comments section of the survey.

I had a friend named Doug who exemplified the complexity of the autism spectrum and illustrated the limits of set categorization. Unlike me, who could pass for normal, Doug was ostensibly autistic with an overly formal manner (he initiated every phone conversation by stating his full name) and a monotone voice. He also had difficulty with figurative language and implied meanings. I remember seeing the movie *Pulp Fiction* with him in the theater, and as explicit and graphic as the movie was, there were still undertones I needed to explain to Doug. But before I could jump to the conclusion that this was an obvious example of me being the high-functioning one, I needed to remember that I would never have been at the theater in the first place if Doug hadn't driven me.

Whereas Doug had been driving since he was 16, I had never been able to learn regardless of how many times I tried. And, to further complicate matters, Doug may have been a literal thinker, but that didn't stop him from engaging in imaginative play. When Doug was a kid, he'd entertain himself while shoveling snow by pretending that the shovel was a microphone and he was performing on stage.

Where I learned the most about myself and my autism was in working with other autistics. As part of an independent project pursued under the auspices of Professor Rossman, I worked as an intern at a day program for developmentally disabled adults called Midway Training Services (MTS). Our clients lived in local group homes and institutions and would come to the day program to complete what was known as contract work which usually amounted to filling, sealing, and placing labels on envelopes. My job was that of work supervisor, though the severity of my clients' disabilities often had me playing the role of orderly and hall monitor—helping people feed themselves and escorting them to the bathroom, cleaning up after spills and other messes, and anticipating and de-escalating meltdowns.

Many of my clients were autistic, and in observing them, I saw many aspects of myself. There was the client who could not tolerate any uncertainty and required a complete accounting of what was going to happen in his day. And any alteration in the schedule was treated as the worst type of betrayal. That could almost have been a description of me. As much as I prided myself on my ability to be spontaneous, I had to concede that there were times when I'd default to a mindset of inflexibility and rigidity.

There was the client who, like me, would self-stim with language. He'd repeat stock phrases out loud like "go to the bathroom, have to go to the bathroom…no don't have to go," an utterance that, as a staff person responsible for his care, left me in a bit of a quandary until I learned that that was just something he said. I have many stock phrases of my own—lines from books and TV shows or snippets of casual conversations that have burrowed themselves into my consciousness and remerge like that earworm of a catchy tune that you just can't get out of your head. I try to keep my linguistic self-stimming to a minimum and to myself, only fully indulging in it when I'm alone and in private. Someone like me being wire-tapped by the CIA or FBI with frustrated agents trying to crack the code behind my random utterances would make a great comedy.

Then there were the clients who taught me about the broader human condition and demonstrated the truth in autism writer Donna Willliams' quip that "autism is normal with the volume turned way up." I was particularly enlightened by the client who, in the middle of December, would constantly ask about the Minnesota State Fair, an event that didn't occur until August. One day it occurred to me that her anxiety might be assuaged by looking at pictures of the State Fair. A co-worker put together a picture book for the client to look at whenever she started to obsess about the State Fair, and it seemed to do the trick. A similar strategy worked when we gave her a Christmas toy in anticipation of the holiday season. That's when it hit me—aren't we all comforted by pictures and other mementos of pleasant experiences? My client's eccentricity was an expression of a completely normal proclivity.

MTS's clients were considered the hardcore of the disability community. Society had pretty much given up on them. But, as severe as their disabilities were, and as much as I myself was often impacted by having to tend to them, I couldn't help but see some of their redeeming qualities. There was a sense of humor, consideration of and kindness towards others, and even (despite the co-morbidity with intellectual disability) a touch of ingenuity. For instance, most of my clients couldn't read, but, as I mentioned earlier, they had to place labels on envelopes. How did they know which way was right side up? They determined that by looking at the shape of the text.

While working at MTS, I coined the phrase "turning tendencies into talents" to express my goal of channeling autistic behaviors into more socially appropriate and useful activities. My mom loved the phrase, though I think she interpreted it a bit differently than I did. My mom focused on the word "talent" and saw my project as unearthing hidden abilities. And, while I did try to turn one of my clients into a poet by recording her stream-of-consciousness manner of communicating, the "talents" I was in search of were not necessarily so lofty. I had one client, for instance, who was obsessively clean to the point that he would engage in the decidedly unclean behavior of pica or the picking up of nonedible items from the environment and placing them in his mouth. What if I could help him translate his impulse to clean into actually cleaning? Whenever I saw him engaging in pica, I'd hand him a rag and encourage him to wipe the area that seemed to have captured his attention. The endeavor was moderately successful in that I was able to get my client to sometimes reach for the rag without my prompting.

Outside of MTS, I was on the Board of Directors of the Twin Cities Autism Society (TCAS). In fact, the Vice-President of MTS was the President of TCAS, and the Marketing Director of MTS was a fellow board member, a neighbor in the same apartment complex, and my ride to work. I was still in close contact with Jack Rossman and Janet Schank, and as an alumnus of Macalester College, I was always being invited to special events. As a high-functioning autistic who had conducted research on autism, I was in constant demand to speak at conferences and at schools; I was even once interviewed by a high school student writing a paper on autism.

I was also living on my own. Well, I wasn't completely on my own. The apartment I lived in was one of two condos recently purchased by my mother and my grandfather. My mother owned the one on the ground floor, and my grandfather owned the one on the second floor. When my mother received a postdoc at UCLA and moved back to Los Angeles, she rented out her apartment. I stayed in St. Paul and occupied the apartment my grandfather bought but never actually lived in. My mother and I spoke on the phone every night, and she made frequent trips back to Minnesota to check on me. I also flew back to LA to visit her. The main reason for my remaining in St. Paul was to finish up the 3.5 credits I needed to earn my BA, though since it involved writing a paper, I could easily have done that from LA. The main incentives for staying in St. Paul were the job at MTS and a woman named Anne.

I met Anne at a Twin Cities Autism Society Annual Conference, where I was participating in a panel discussion with other autistic adults. I took this opportunity to hand out my questionnaire to members of the audience, which included Anne and her mother. It turned out that Anne had just been diagnosed with Asperger's Syndrome a week earlier, but autism was not the only thing we had in common. She had graduated from Macalester College two years earlier, and I was set to graduate that June.

Anne's autism didn't come with a learning disability, and unlike me, she was excellent in math. In fact, she conceptualized what separated the autistic from the non-autistic in geometric terms. Anne agreed with my assessment that no one, autistic or not, could lay claim to having arrived at psychosocial perfection; however, if psychosocial perfection could be viewed as a point in space, Anne suggested, "we veer off this way, and normal people veer off that way." Anne and I also shared what you might call a propensity towards sensory build-up and overload. Once we were returning from a weekend trip to Wisconsin to visit some of her extended family, and she described feeling grimy and sticky and anxious to get back to her apartment. I didn't happen to feel that way at the moment, but I knew exactly what she was talking about. And, like me, Anne had an image in her head of what an "itch" actually looked like.

Like I was with my mom, Anne was very close to her parents. Indeed, it was Anne's mother who, in a way, initiated and greenlit our relationship. When the two women first approached me, Anne's mother started the conversation, and, at least according to what Anne later told me, her mother's response to my presentation was to say, "oh, just wrap him up and take him home." Anne's father was an anesthesiologist who loved to engage me and everyone else in philosophical discourse. He had an extensive collection of exotic liquors, spirits, and wines that he'd share with guests before starting a conversation with his favorite opener "so, do you have any insights?" In addition to introducing me to the finest in his library of libations, Anne's father also lent me a book on the brain and gave me a copy of one of his old medical journals.

Anne's parents lived in a rustic-looking house, perched on a hill overlooking a residential tree-lined street. The house reminded me of the one in the famous Mount Rushmore scene of the movie *North by Northwest*. When the weather was not conducive to sitting out on the balcony and contemplating the meaning of it all, which in Minnesota was most of the time, Anne's family would take me out for dinner. And, when my mother was in town, she'd come along too.

It was a nice little life that could very well have continued, but then opportunity knocked. My mother got a fellowship to do research at Harvard's W.E.B. Du Bois Institute and she invited me to come with her.

I had a decision to make. Anne told me right off that she did not believe in long-distance relationships, so I knew I couldn't have my girlfriend and the Harvard experience too. My mother knew what the best course of action was for me, and it didn't take much for her to strengthen my resolve. As happy as I was living in St. Paul, I didn't see much of a future in it. I was feeling unfulfilled at MTS, and even my co-workers felt I had far more to contribute to the field of autism than performing menial tasks at a day program. In fact, when I made my final decision to move to Cambridge, and I'd resigned from MTS, the Vice-President reportedly said, "Gyasi is too talented for this job."

The plan was for me to write my memoirs. Following in the tradition of both the slave narrative and the autistic narrative, I would tell my life story and call it <u>Incidents in the Life of an Autistic, Written by Himself</u> riffing off Harriet Jacobs' <u>Incidents in the Life of a Slave Girl, Written by Herself</u>. The intellectual community of Harvard seemed like the perfect environment in which to complete that task. I now only had to inform Anne. I'd hoped she'd make an exception to her ban on long-distance relationships or, at the very least, remain my girlfriend until I moved to Cambridge, which wasn't for another few months. She did neither. In what probably remains one of the most civilized break-ups in human history, Anne and I parted as romantic partners but remained friends.

Chapter Seven:
The Life Of The Mind

I t was a scene brimming with symbolism. I was on my way to see Dr. BJ Freeman, the autism expert who had diagnosed me as mentally retarded; and in order to get to her office, I had to cross the lobby of the psychiatric hospital where I had once been a patient. However, the reason for my visit was not for a psychiatric appointment or a neuropsychological evaluation, as had usually been the case when I spoke to mental health professionals in the past; I was simply stopping by a brain doctor's office for a friendly chat.

At the time of my visit with Dr. Freeman, I had succeeded in accomplishing many of the things that I was never supposed to accomplish. I had lived on my own, held down a full-time job, been involved in romantic relationships, and graduated from college. In fact, I was about to discuss research I had conducted on autism as a psychology major in college with the very person who had predicted that I would never make it beyond the sixth grade.

As much as I was looking forward to the encounter, I was also a little apprehensive. My history with UCLA Neuropsychiatric Institute was a contentious one. When I was a patient there, I was seen as an angry, unstable teenager; and my objections to situations were often dismissed as simply the product of my tendency to blow things out of proportion. Even though I had never interacted with Dr. Freeman while in the hospital, I couldn't help but wonder if my reputation didn't precede me and wouldn't, therefore, color how she reacted to my criticisms of autism discourse.

A lot had changed since my hospitalizations 6 years earlier; whereas I had once nursed a deep distrust of mental health professionals, I was now an acolyte of the study of the mind who was actually considering becoming a psychologist. But would Dr. Freeman take me as a true convert? Would she see my criticisms as being born of honest intellectual inquiry or as a residue of my hostility towards authority?

Then there was that thing that Dr. Freeman said in a recent newspaper article about a couple of autistic newlyweds. He was a mathematical savant; she was an accomplished artist and musician. They had both been diagnosed late in life--they were in their forties--and the discovery of their common condition had coincided with them finding each other. But all was not perfect. There were fights about his tendency to put pressure on her and her habit of simply shutting down in response. Dr. Freeman was quoted as attributing this relationship problem to the lack of empathy endemic to autism.

I was so concerned about a negative reaction that I censored my own writing—at least that which I showed to Dr. Freeman. In addition to writing a research paper on autism, I had also kept a journal recounting my experiences working at MTS. Dr. Freeman had asked me to bring a sample of my work to our appointment. I could have easily given her my paper and my journal. However, I was worried about how some of my emotional honesty—particularly in reference to my feelings about problems at MTS—would come across. So, I opted to just give Dr. Freeman my paper, to present her only with my researched and reasoned thoughts about autism.

At my meeting with Dr. Freeman, I discovered that my fears had been unfounded and that, in a way, I had boxed and stereotyped her.

Far from being offended, Dr. Freeman was solicitous of my research and encouraged me to tell my story. Offering me a piece of humble pie, she noted that while she and her colleagues had learned much about autism in the last twenty years, they still had quite a way to go in terms of understanding the disorder. She felt that the perspectives of people like me, who had in many ways overcome autism, would be important sources of information. A poignant moment occurred when Dr. Freeman introduced me to one of her interns, and the latter was inspired to imagine one of the autistic children she worked with growing up and turning out like me.

Dr. Freeman and I had a nice talk. I shared some of the fascinating things I learned about autism in the course of my research. I told her how I was particularly intrigued by the correlations between different autistic symptoms and damage to specific areas of the brain. I even ventured to proffer insights gleaned from my work at MTS. Dr. Freeman told me about her autistic dissertation advisee who was examining the quality of life issues in autism.

We also discussed the autistic couple mentioned earlier. One of the artist's paintings was hanging on Dr. Freeman's wall; it featured an elaborate, intricately drawn, multi-colored design that defied any sort of description except for the one offered by a reviewer assessing the artist in general as "intensively creative." When Dr. Freeman told me the two were having marital problems, I told her about my recent break-up with Anne. She laughed at my suggestion that with relationship problems, we autistics were finally achieving some semblance of normalcy.

- - -

I was all but a part of the Harvard community. My mother was a Resident Fellow at the W.E.B. Du Bois Institute and a Resident Scholar in Currier House. Currier House is one of Harvard's twelve upperclassman dormitories, and as a Resident Scholar, my mother's major obligation was to be a presence; in the dining hall and at the Senior Commons Room, a monthly gathering of people associated with the house. For me, both interacting with students in the dining hall and attending the Senior Commons Room were simply privileges. I was particularly fond of the Senior Commons Room. It was a well-rounded evening, a night of nourishment, complete with a reception, live entertainment, a three-course meal, and a lecture. It fed my mind, my body, and my soul. Then there were the weekly symposia at the W.E.B. Du Bois Institute. After each symposium, my mother, the other Du Bois Fellows, and I would eat lunch at John Harvard's, a local Harvard Square pub. I loved the organized socialization and the intellectual stimulation provided by my involvement with the Harvard community.

I appreciated the unconditional acceptance—no one held it against me that I had no real Harvard affiliation or even raised an eyebrow at the fact that I was a grown man who lived with his mother. My autism was also not a problem. My plan to write my memoirs was greeted with interest and excitement. When I first met Barbara Graham, one of the Masters of Currier House, and I told her about my desire to write my memoirs in order to combat stereotypes, she responded immediately and enthusiastically, "Oh, just like [Harvard sociologist] Sara Lawrence-Lightfoot…you want to use personal narratives to change public policy." At my first Senior Commons Room dinner, I had an engaging conversation about the *Rainman* stereotype with a doctoral candidate in psychology.

In the dining hall one night, I met a student who could have sworn he once knew someone with autism until, after a few seconds of resting his forehead in the palm of his hand, he realized he was thinking about the movie *Rainman*. After recovering from that embarrassing, though humorous, moment, he agreed with me; I could certainly, through my own experience, give the parents of autistic kids hope and maybe even some advice. One of the Du Bois Fellows took me to lunch hoping to get just that type of advice—he knew a couple with a 3 ½-year-old child that had just been diagnosed with "mild" autism.

By attending the weekly symposia, I was getting the benefits of a Harvard education. At least, that's what one of my mother's colleagues said. Equally important, I was contributing to the dialogue in a way that was winning me wide acclaim. At the end of one symposium, Cornel West, a scholar whose way with words I admired to the point of seeing him as the embodiment of intelligence, gave me the ultimate compliment; he said, "I could just see your mind working." I was using my autistic gifts, my verbal ability, and my unique way of seeing the world.

The exact nature of my autistic gifts was codified by a series of neuropsychological tests I took at the University's Health Service. Dr. Kenneth Dinklage was a psychologist who specialized in learning disabilities, and he gave me an IQ test as a way of assessing my cognitive strengths and weaknesses. My verbal abilities were off the charts, while my visual-spatial skills barely registered. I remember my introduction to the Stroop Test, a real mind-bender that has you reading a color word like "red," but instead of saying "red," you must say the color of the font the three letters are printed in. The Stroop Test is a test of attention, and as Dr. Dinklage noted in the final report, and as I can attest, I was barely able to even complete the exam.

As much as the Stroop Test frustrated me, it also fascinated me. I even wondered if it could be a form of mental exercise. But Dr. Dinklage felt I'd be better served by focusing on my strengths, my large vocabulary, and my way with words. Indeed, by giving me the space to write my autobiography, my mother was already steps ahead of this medical advice. My mom had me enroll in a writing course at the Harvard Extension School. She knew me well enough to know that I respond positively to structure, so taking a class that required at least 60 pages by the end of the semester would all but guarantee that I would produce something.

What my mom (or I, for that matter) could not have anticipated was the extent of my capacity for writer's block. Along with structure, the class came with a teacher and classmates who were interested in my story. Unfortunately, I couldn't tell it. I had trouble organizing my thoughts. My mother had told me to write a series of incidents, but I couldn't decide which incidents to choose or whether something was an incident or a series of related events. And how should I best sequence them, chronologically or thematically? Should I break the book up into separate documents or create one master document?

I'd get bogged down in mechanics or in what my mom called "formatting." I also had the terrible tendency to edit while I wrote. I couldn't bear to see something that wasn't perfect printed on the page. Conversely, once I had written something, I'd get stuck on it and find it impossible to see beyond it. Another problem was my shame at some of the behaviors that led to my autism diagnosis.

As much as I was haunted by my past, a person in my present made me fear for my future. The ubiquitous Brother Blue, aka., Hugh Morgan Hill; an eccentric, highly verbal presence at most Harvard events who always dressed in blue (hence his moniker). A light-skinned African American man in his mid to late 60s, Brother Blue, could have been an older version of me. I didn't have any ill feelings towards Brother Blue; I liked him. It's just that I also worried that I was him. Though I later learned that Brother Blue was a professional storyteller with a couple of Ivy League degrees—not even close to being the failure I'd constructed in my mind--the man I encountered when I first came to Cambridge in 1997 was like an apparition from my future, a future filled with intellectual aspirations but no real accomplishments.

Like me, Brother Blue's presence was valued. Every Du Bois Institute Symposium ended with an opportunity for Brother Blue to deliver a soliloquy, a ritual that was greeted by regular attendees of the weekly Symposia with anticipation, and once, when a distinguished presenter refused to allow Brother Blue time to speak, the slight was later reflected upon with outrage. But, as I also feared was the case with me, Brother Blue's affiliation, his "right to hang," was considered, at best, ambiguous. At a dinner for Du Bois Fellows, the Institute's director, Henry Louis Gates, Jr., gave the history behind Brother Blue's weekly orations.

When Gates became the Director of the Institute in 1991, he encountered Brother Blue during the question-and-answer period of the weekly symposia. Since Blue was given to long-windedness, Gates decided to give the former his own designated slot—the slot right after everyone else in the audience had had an opportunity to respond to the speaker. After telling this story, Gates recounted how surprised he was when he discovered that Blue had a Ph.D. from Harvard and went on to speculate that this possibly brilliant man must have at some point in his life made a decision, "for whatever reason," to just stop producing.

Gates could have been talking about me. Professor Gates, himself, would joke that I could be the next W.E.B. Du Bois. My mind would run with it. One thing I liked about Du Bois was his concept of double consciousness, the dual awareness that African Americans have of how they see themselves versus how they are perceived by society. The idea of a double consciousness could easily be applied to autistics. What if I called my book The Souls of Autistic Folk playing off the Du Bois classic The Souls of Black Folk? I'd be the autistic W.E.B. Du Bois.

But, in truth, I knew that I was no scholar. I was no W.E.B. Du Bois. Even though I graduated with honors from Macalester College, I felt that I was not academically inclined. I had always had problems in school, and I was neither a fast nor a voracious reader. I would also block when it came to writing which, of course, I was doing while hovering on the outskirts of Harvard's intellectual community. So, at the dinner where Professor Gates recounted the story of meeting this possibly brilliant man who just stopped producing, I asked, in jest, if I could one day take the latter's place. I wouldn't be the next W.E.B. Du Bois—I'd be the next Brother Blue.

Without completely abandoning the idea that I'd one day write my memoirs, my mom and I looked for other ways for me to find my place in the world and make a living. Having fallen in love with campus life, I started applying for staff and research positions at Harvard and other colleges and universities in the greater Boston area. I also applied to the Master's program at the Harvard Graduate School of Education not because I was interested in teaching but because I was drawn to the work of psychologist Howard Gardner, one of the school's professors, and his theory of multiple intelligences. My mom and I also hoped I could parley an advanced degree in Education into a career as an autism consultant. Most of my application letters went unanswered (though I did get some interviews), and I was rejected by the Graduate School of Education. I worked briefly as an aide to an autistic man who lived with his elderly mother, but the job that I got that suited me the most was as a bookseller at the Harvard Coop, a branch of the Barnes & Noble bookstore located in the heart of Harvard Square.

Working at the Coop seemed like the ideal job. I relished working in an intellectually stimulating environment surrounded by books. My mother appreciated the fact that the Harvard Shuttle stopped directly in front of Currier House and dropped me off almost right across the street from the Coop. And Dr. Dinklage felt that interacting with customers would keep me socially engaged.

My mother and I were surfing the Web one day when we came across the Graduate School of Library and Information Science at Simmons College. I don't remember what drew us to Simmons, but the description of the library program sounded perfect. The work of a reference librarian in a library seemed almost indistinguishable from my job as a customer service representative at a bookstore. However, whereas I could hardly expect to earn a living doing the latter, the former seemed to have real career potential

What my mom and I discovered was more serendipitous than either of us could have imagined. It turned out that Barbara Graham wasn't just the co-master of Currier House. Her day job was as a Harvard University Library administrator. She had gotten her library degree from Simmons. Another Simmons alumnus was a Harvard reference librarian named Steve Love, who worked at Hilles Library (right next door to Currier House) and had helped my mom with her research. I interviewed both Barbara and Steve about librarianship, and Barbara even looked over my personal statement. During our investigation, my mom and I found that we had other acquaintances who had worked as librarians at Harvard after having passed through Simmons.

Librarianship would turn out to be very different than either my mom or I could ever have imagined, and it would take my life in a very different direction. I never saw myself as technically or scientifically inclined. If there was a domain that suited me, it was in the arts or humanities. Yet, the field of librarianship at the turn of the 21st century was very much equivalent to a type of applied computer science; gone were the days of card catalogs; now, it was all about digital databases and electronic records. And then there was the ubiquitous World Wide Web, which inspired both fear and loathing in many librarians. Part of my education as a library student was learning about these new technologies while confronting the impact they would have on my chosen profession.

The first book I read in library school was Professor Smith's 40-plus page syllabus. The class was Reference and Information Services, and it was one of the first steps on my road to becoming a librarian. Like Mount Everest to an aspiring rock-climber, the syllabus looked both imposing and exciting. In addition to stating such lofty goals as "students will leave the class having developed their own philosophy of reference," the syllabus listed 100 or so reference questions to be answered over the course of the semester with an equal number of reference sources to be physically examined. I remember thinking, "if I succeed in doing all this, I will have achieved badness."

From the beginning, Smith's goals were clear: not only did he want to maintain the august traditions of librarianship in the face of new technology, but also, he wanted to up the intellectual caliber of a field that he feared was a bit of an academic fifth wheel. He opened the first class with a "those who can do, those who can't" joke, replacing "teach" with "become librarians." He'd spend an entire class disparaging the course textbook as too elementary. The books he wanted us to read, one of which was no longer in print, were far more scholarly, and he recommended that every student read them before graduating from Simmons.

Like his syllabus, Professor Smith had a commanding presence that was both intimidating and inspiring. A 6 ft. tall man with snow-white hair, wire-rimmed glasses, and a tomato red complexion, Professor Smith looked like a professor. His usual wardrobe of a sports coat, collared shirt (sometimes accentuated with a bow tie), and slacks gave him an almost ivy-league demeanor. I remember once overhearing two female students refer to him as being "Paul Newman cute." In the classroom, Professor Smith was all charm as he entertained with anecdotes and dazzled with erudition. Outside of the classroom, he was formal and stiff, and God help you if you imposed on his personal space. I once approached Professor Smith after a class only to be abruptly brushed off; the engaging professor had already shed his teaching persona.

I had the misfortune of experiencing more of the out-of-class Smith than the in-class Smith, and I think it might have had something to do with my request for academic accommodations.

Librarianship was already on shaky intellectual ground—now I come along presenting with a cognitive disability! I'm sure I didn't help matters when I had difficulty mastering the ins and outs of a complex (and what a classmate described as being too math-based) database the class was required to use.

My first semester at Simmons was not a successful one. I just missed being placed on academic probation; as the Assistant Dean put it, "you're still okay—your name didn't come up at the faculty meeting." My morale was as bruised as my GPA, and I strongly considered dropping out of library school. Then, I got an important phone call from the American Library Association--I had won a Spectrum Initiative Fellowship, a fellowship designed to increase the number of librarians of color that my mother had encouraged me to apply for towards the beginning of the semester. The fellowship had already started to work; I had a renewed sense of purpose and hope. Along with reinvigorated confidence in my ability to be a librarian, the fellowship also garnered me respect from an unexpected source— Professor Smith. Although I never took a class with Smith again, I got to see a great deal of his in-class personality. For my remaining year and a half at Simmons, Smith always greeted me in the halls with a smile and a nod.

I took a five-day summer school course called Technical Services with Professor Oyler. Technical Services is not about computers. It refers to those library functions such as cataloging and collection development that the public never sees, analogous to the movement of props and sets in a theatrical performance. Professor Oyler was a towering figure both literally and figuratively. Standing at about 6 feet tall, Professor Oyler had a reputation as "The Grand Matron of Technical Services." Professor Oyler's unassuming dress of loose-fitting blouses and pants suits contrasted sharply with her booming, baritone voice that sometimes dipped into a monotone. If I hadn't known better, I would have thought she, too, was autistic.

Autistic or not, Professor Oyler made me feel like I belonged. She had no objection to me having a note-taker, even though she, herself, supplied the class with copious notes and a voluminous number of handouts. And, because the class met daily from 9-5 and Professor Oyler recognized that no one was going to be up to writing after eight hours of lecture, the due date for the final paper was set for two weeks after the summer session ended. So, in essence, everyone was given extra time; I was just given a little bit more—three weeks.

Like my mom had suggested I do with my psychology major in college, she encouraged me to make autism a part of my final project for the technical services class. So, I did an examination of the Cambridge Public Library's collections in the area of autism, which was not particularly extensive though they did have a plethora of electronic resources made readily available to the public.

I took Cataloging with Oyler the following fall, and, again, she proved quite accommodating—even agreeing to meet with me in-between classes to clarify things I didn't understand. Most importantly, my accommodations came with no stigma attached. In fact, a small study group formed around me and another disabled student in the class, and we all would meet in the library before every exam—when the non-disabled students would go off to class to take the exam, it was treated like the most natural thing that the other disabled student and I stayed behind so that we could have extra time.

My last year at Simmons was a highlight in my library science education. As part of a course called Bibliographic Instruction and Methods with Professor Shoemaker, I was able to combine my interests in psychology and African American studies. Professor Shoemaker was a middle-aged, unassuming woman, both in manner and dress, with white short-cropped hair. Like her doppelganger Jessica Fletcher on the old television series *Murder, She Wrote*, Professor Shoemaker had lived on the sidelines of crime—she once taught sociology in a prison. The thrust of the course I took with her was on learning theory and, our major project was to design a teaching module based on the best teaching practices.

I demonstrated how the Encarta Africana Encyclopedia CD-ROM was an effective teaching tool because its multimedia features engaged multiple modalities and catered to different learning styles. Indeed, I had wanted to trace the history of the Encarta Africana Encyclopedia during my first semester at Simmons, but Professor Smith nixed it, saying that my idea was too contemporary to be worthy of scholarly consideration. He failed to grasp that the CD-ROM was only new in form, not in content; it was the culmination of an Encyclopedia begun by W.E.B. Du Bois in 1909 to document the accomplishments of the African diaspora.

The summer before I graduated from Simmons, I went to two library conferences that made me look forward to becoming a librarian. As part of my Spectrum Initiative Fellowship, I participated in a three-day Leadership Institute at Hamburger University in Oak Brook, IL. The Institute was immediately followed by the American Library Association's (ALA) annual conference in Chicago.

My mother accompanied me to both conferences, and no one cast any aspersions at me for being a grown man traveling with his mother. In fact, my mom fit in perfectly. At the Institute, she was even allowed to attend some of the sessions, and during the downtime between meetings my mom was readily included in all conversations. As my mother explained to one of the organizers of the Institute, she came with me to provide support. An explanation really wasn't necessary; in fact, my mom told the organizer this while the three of us were hanging out in Chicago during the ALA conference.

While in Chicago, I went to a Technical Services breakfast in which I sat at a table with Professor Oyler. She was pleased when I told her of her reputation as "The Grand Matron of Technical Services." At an event on black librarianship, my mom and I ran into an old acquaintance from the W.E.B. Du Bois Institute. Howard

Dodson was the head of the Schomberg Center, the Harlem Branch of the New York Public Library, and we had met him when he came to visit Harvard. When his plane was delayed, the three of us hung out in our apartment in Currier House. We talked about everything from the history of the black migration north to what autistic neologisms revealed about the nature of language. As the author Zora Neale Hurston would have put it, we "passed nations through our mouths," and, from what I remember, the journey lasted for hours. So, seeing Howard at the ALA conference was very much like running into an old friend, and one of the first things he said upon seeing my mom and me referred right back to the evening we'd spent together a couple of years earlier: "Did you guys ever manage to get any sleep that night?"

By the time my mom and I returned to Cambridge, librarianship was no longer just a plan B, the "those who can do, those who can't" scenario suggested by Smith or, as I would sometimes think in my darkest moments, "God's punishment for not having completed my memoirs." No, I was more enthusiastic than ever about entering the profession, and I was looking forward to my job interview for a position as a library assistant for the Harvard College Library. I still hoped one day to finish my memoirs; being a librarian would just add to my story.

Chapter Eight:
The World Of Work

Nine days after I started working in the Office of Technical Services at Lamont, one of Harvard's undergraduate libraries, the Head of Technical Services, my direct supervisor, abruptly resigned, setting in motion a cascade of events that would force a reckoning between my autism and my ability to work. But, at first, as shocked and disoriented as I was, I felt charged with a sense of inclusion and purpose when the library head sent out a series of e-mails to all employees. The e-mails were not simply testimonials to my supervisor and to all the great things she had accomplished during her twenty-seven years as Head of Technical Services; they were calls to collective action. The library head welcomed me and some other recent hires and thanked everyone for coping during this time of transition; she also promised that the search committee would be asking for everyone's input and that a new Head of Technical Services would be in place by November. In the meantime, the Library's most immediate goal was the order and receipt of materials for course reserves.

I could identify with the positive characterization of my supervisor even though our working relationship was fleeting. Over the next couple of weeks after relocating to the Office of Information

Systems, my supervisor would make intermittent visits to the Office of Technical Services and send out periodic e-mails. Then, her new job became more involved, and all communication essentially stopped. But the great things said about my former boss rang true for me; I found her to be organized and logical, yet flexible and reasonable. Her detailed instructions on how to carry out certain procedures lent clarity to complex tasks that is usually impossible to accomplish with words alone. She was patient as I assimilated the material, and, equally important, she was encouraging.

My co-workers in the Office of Technical Services did not concur with my positive evaluation of the former supervisor. The new cataloger compared his brief stint working with her to being held at gunpoint: "She trains from the other end of an M-16." My other office mates agreed; according to them, their old boss was very particular about how she wanted things done, and she was even more insistent on what things only she could do. I could identify with my co-worker's descriptions of this rigidity and anal retentiveness. I even added to the office lore by sharing the story about the time I was told to not keep a Styrofoam coffee cup too close to the computer even though the cup was covered, and the time I was reminded, "' i' before 'e' except after 'c,'" when I was caught making a typo. I noticed the quirks, but they didn't particularly bother me.

My displeasure came in her absence when her tendency to be hands-on backfired on me. Because she had done so many things herself, and she left before an adequate replacement could be found, I was left with no supervision. On paper, I was covered. The Associate Librarian took over as the Interim Head of Technical Services; however, he said he knew nothing about Technical Services. In recognition of this fact, he appointed the new cataloger Workflow Supervisor, but, alas, he was an even newer employee than me.

As for the quarter-century worth of experience working in the Office of Technical Services shared among my other office mates, little of it was useful to me. Again, the old boss had been a domineering presence, and for the six months that my position had been vacant before I arrived, she had basically done the job herself. Fortunately, she had also left a paper trail, one that I was able to follow when things came up that were not covered during my brief training period.

But my greatest asset was my mother. She had once worked as a management analyst for the state of California, and she applied her skills to many aspects of my job. She helped me break down my job duties into manageable chunks, get organized by creating a filing system, and even coached me in my interactions with co-workers. My mother's behind-the-scenes work went a long way to guide me through this period of transition. But she wasn't completely invisible. At a staff picnic held in a small garden next to the library, my mother had an opportunity to meet my officemates and hear from both the head of the library and Associate Librarian what a pleasure I was to work with and how well I was bearing up under the pressure. Things were stressful, but I felt good. I was confident that I was doing a good job. After the picnic, my mother suggested that no one I worked with would probably ever guess that I was autistic.

November came, and there was no new Head of Technical Services. November was also the month of my three-month probationary review, which I passed, but not before being completely castigated by the Associate Librarian in his written evaluation. After acknowledging that I completed my probationary period under extremely unusual circumstances, he took me to task for not being able to prioritize because of a pile of invoices left in the in-box.

In addition to being unable to prioritize, I was accused of causing my co-workers undue stress and anxiety. The evaluation was a jolt but not a complete surprise because of the type of evaluations I had received in the past. At MTS, I had been given all "3's" on a scale from "1" to "5" because my supervisor wanted to make a statement about grade inflation. Alluding to Garrison Keillor's joke about the town where everyone is above average, my supervisor explained to me that there is nothing wrong with being average. And, certainly, I was far from a perfect employee. As was pointed out to me, and I had to concede was true, I often seemed at a loss as to what to do next as if I were waiting for someone to direct me, which "was never going to happen."

My supervisor at the Harvard Coop also gave me all "3's" on a "1" to "5" scale, which particularly galled my mom because of the way in which my reliability as an employee was constantly being exploited. When I first started working at the Coop, I was given something that is rather unusual in retail; a set 8 am to 5 pm schedule that just so happened to coincide nicely with when the Harvard Shuttle ran. When my hiring supervisor resigned, my set schedule reverted to the retail standard of week-to-week variability. Though for me, there was not much variability; my new supervisor consistently gave me the Friday and Saturday late-night closing shifts because, as my mom pointed out, I could be counted on to be there.

While I enjoyed the late shift and found the nighttime quiet particularly serene, my mom was far more practical. The Coop closed long after the Harvard Shuttle stopped running, which meant my mom had to pick me up from work. So, when my supervisor gave me all "3s" on my evaluation, my mom encouraged me to question the results, arguing that people have different strengths and weaknesses and, therefore, cannot be across the board "average" in all areas. I succeeded in getting my supervisor to admit that my customer service skills were excellent, but she countered that since excellent customer service was expected, my performance was still average. That left me speechless. For years I thought this reasoning was unique; then I read The Caine Mutiny, a 1951 novel about sailors who mutiny against their captain during WWII. At one point in the novel, the captain asserts: "Excellent performance is standard. Standard performance is sub-standard. And sub-standard performance is not permitted to exist."

Because of the capricious nature of my past job performance evaluations, I had a difficult time taking the whole concept of job evaluations seriously. They seemed to be more a reflection of my lack of assertiveness than anything else. So, the Associate Librarian's words were disappointing and hurtful but finally not surprising. My mom even suggested that he had to justify the need for a Head of Technical Services. What better way than to show that the job wasn't being done adequately? But my mom also stressed that if he said things that were wrong, I needed to correct the record. Fortunately, the probationary process gave me an opportunity to write a rebuttal that would be included with my original evaluation.

My mother helped me write the rebuttal, and when I met with the Associate Librarian to discuss it, he agreed completely with the points I made. He recognized that he had made a mistake in confusing statements for invoices, and he also understood that part of one of my co-worker's jobs was to devote some time to assisting me in ordering and receiving books. He also agreed that a lot of my time was being taken up because of the absence of student workers. Everything seemed to be fine.

In March, a new Head of Technical Services was finally hired. In recognition of my having worked with no supervision for 6 months and the fact that I was in my last semester at Simmons, my new supervisor treated me more like a librarian than a library assistant. She lobbied to have my position reclassified from paraprofessional to professional only to be informed that a similar request had already been made to human resources and rejected.

Nonetheless, I was still treated like a professional. In what I read as a genuine sign of respect, my supervisor asked me to do some of her work as a favor. Specifically, she asked me to complete the end of the fiscal year accounting due to Book Accounts which, incidentally, I found required very little actual math. I was also sent, along with the cataloger, to a conference at Boston College put on by Yankee Book Peddler, one of our library's major book suppliers. All three of us (my supervisor, the cataloger, and I) went to a Technical Services conference at the College of the Holy Cross in Worchester. My mother drove me to the train station, I took the commuter rail to meet my supervisor near where she lived in Beverly, and she drove me the rest of the way to the conference, where we met up with the cataloger. Incidentally, I was driven home by Professor Oyler, who just happened to also be at the conference.

As good as I felt about my working relationship with the new supervisor, the probationary evaluation was always in the back of my mind. How would my supervisor react to it if she read it? I knew I had my rebuttal, but as my mom pointed out, it was a response to the Associate Librarian whose initial statement would probably carry more weight. My supervisor assured me, when I asked her, that she had not read the evaluation, and even if she had, it would have no impact on how she saw me. I was somewhat mollified until her attitude towards me seemed to change.

It started soon after I finished the financial housecleaning for book accounts. My supervisor noticed a stack of general collection orders piling up on my desk. General collection orders didn't have the same urgency as orders for course reserves, but my supervisor was just bothered by the sheer volume that had accumulated. She started to accuse me of having difficulty "shifting priorities." She went so far as to call herself my overseer, which my mom read as having racial overtones. I wasn't so sure. After all, Harvard does have a Board of Overseers; the comment struck me more as an inadvertent reference to the Associate Librarian's stated opinion that I was an employee who needed a great deal of oversight.

Whatever my supervisor meant by calling herself my overseer, in practical terms, it amounted to me having to show her all my work.

She didn't even like me putting things in file folders; she referred to my attempts at organization as "hiding pending work." She'd make me meet with her each morning to tell her what I planned to do that day. Because she did not have her own office, our morning meetings took place in a private conference room. Being pulled away from my co-workers for special attention was reminiscent of my partial mainstreaming in 4th grade, where I'd be separated from my regular classroom for certain periods.

Even before I'd noticed this change in my supervisor, I'd spoken with human resources and my union rep about the possibility of getting the Associate Librarian to rewrite my three-month review. My mother and I thought I should cover my bases, particularly as the time for my annual review in August approached. Whereas Human Resources didn't think the Associate Librarian could change my review, my union rep told me I had a right to ask, but he could refuse. The Associate Librarian agreed to rewrite my probationary review, and my supervisor put off my annual review until the revision was completed.

After a couple of months, the Associate Librarian told my supervisor to stop waiting on him before conducting my Annual Review. The Annual Review was different than the 3-month one. The 3-month review was pure narrative; the Associate Librarian wrote a narrative about me, and I wrote a narrative in response—both were placed in my Personnel file. The Annual Review was broken into sections of short-answer questions to be answered by my supervisor and me. The first section was an agreement about job duties and performance standards. The second and third sections were my and my supervisor's summaries, respectively.

As the rules dictated, I got to see my supervisor's summary before filling out my own, and contrary to what I feared, her evaluation of me was relatively positive. She commended me for having worked without supervision for 6 months, for having helped to train her and taking on some of her tasks, and for having established good relationships with book vendors. Her areas for improvement were that I be more social and that I shift priorities better. The admonition about shifting priorities had to do with the mishap regarding the general collection orders, and her statement about me needing to be more social referred to her wish that I consult everyone in the office before sending a student worker to a local bookstore. I hadn't told anyone at Lamont about my autism, but with the dropping of phrases like "be more social" and "shift priorities," I sometimes wondered if they somehow knew.

As much as I liked my job, I had my own concerns. In addition to singling me out as needing helicopter supervision, my supervisor had my desk moved away from the window and placed it so that my back was facing everyone else in the office. The stated reason for moving my desk was that I'd be closer to where the book boxes were delivered so that I could open them. Whenever I'd mention that opening boxes was not part of my job, my supervisor always pointed to the "other related duties" clause in my job description.

Another concern I had was regarding the daily meetings. They were a colossal waste of time. Even though my supervisor claimed they were an opportunity for me to learn how to prioritize from her example, they basically amounted to me reciting what I planned to do that day. And, in terms of my supervisor's opinion about my ability to prioritize, she'd waffle between it being her feeling that I needed to work on it to there being a perception in the library that I needed to work on it. I could never pin her down about who the people were behind this perception, but she did offer that she needed to meet with me in order to counter it.

When it came time for me to write my part of the Annual Review, my mother stressed how important it was that I put my concerns on the record. When I laid out my objections in my staff summary, my supervisor didn't like it. She responded by adding an addendum to her evaluation in which she expressed her displeasure with my uncooperativeness and forecasted just how much progress I, with my drive and intelligence, could make if I'd only listen to her. A meeting was set up with Human Resources; my supervisor called it mediation.

But mediation was a whole different process that occurred outside of the university, a fact I discovered when my union rep just happened to call me to see how things were going. When I mentioned the upcoming meeting, my union rep told me that I needed an advocate because the Human Resources representative my supervisor and I were scheduled to see was not a neutral party; he was management. My union rep offered to accompany me to the meeting, but I'd need to change the date in order to accommodate her schedule.

I wrote a message to my supervisor informing her that not only was the upcoming meeting not mediation, but also the Human Resources representative we were going to see was not a neutral party. I needed to have my own advocate, and the meeting would have to be rescheduled so I could bring my union rep. My supervisor became impatient, writing back to me that we had to get this done as soon as possible. When I wrote back asking, "Why the rush?" she ran over to my desk and told me I knew this had to be resolved quickly, to which I reiterated my question, "why?" In response, my supervisor ordered me to follow her up to the conference room where we had been meeting and, when we entered the room, exclaimed, "I can't take this anymore" as she threw her daily planner down on the table. I apologized for the delay but explained what I had just learned from my union rep. I then asked her why she hadn't told me, and when she said she didn't know, I suggested she should have.

I don't remember exactly what happened next. At some point, my supervisor told me to leave. Thinking I had just been fired, I asked her what she meant by "leave." She said calmly, "Go back to your desk." About fifteen or so minutes later, I got an e-mail apology from my supervisor saying she shouldn't have met with me when she was upset. After all of that, the meeting was rescheduled and took place in a vacant office at Lamont Library between my supervisor, my union rep, someone from Human Resources, and myself.

The basic conclusion from this first meeting was that my supervisor and I had very different working styles—I was deliberative, and she was reactive. It was decided that my supervisor would come up with some performance standards for discussion at the next meeting. She sent me her proposed standards, and though I read them over, it never occurred to me that I needed to respond to them in writing. If I had recognized this and had shared the document with my mother, she would have helped me. She did help me, but unfortunately, I didn't show her the document until the night before the next scheduled meeting. When my mother chastised me for my lapse in judgment and emphasized how crucial it was for me to write a detailed response, I lost it. I yelled, "why do I have to do all this damn work to be a fucking clerk!" Then I did something that I hadn't done since I was a teenager—I banged my head against the wall. When I'd calmed down, my mother and I were up all night responding to my supervisor's document.

At the meeting the next day, as we were going through my detailed responses to the proposed standards, the Human Resources representative interrupted and accused me of questioning my supervisor too much. He said that she did not have to explain herself to me. She could just sit me down and tell me what to do. Disgusted with my attitude and the fact that I was way out of line, the Human Resources representative led my supervisor out of the room and said they'd return later. I don't know how long they were gone; a document written later about the incident cited 45 minutes which sounds perfectly plausible. However long it was, it gave my union rep plenty of time to take me to task for being nitpicky and too particular with language. She even went so far as to suggest that my educational background and the fact that my mother was an English professor made me overly concerned with the way things were phrased, while my supervisor, herself, admitted that she was not very good at saying what she meant.

The Human Resources rep and my supervisor returned, and the meeting ended with an agreement that each day would begin with "stand up meetings" in which the Technical Services staff could discuss the allocation of student workers. The next day, however, there was no "stand-up meeting," and my supervisor criticized me for not having grabbed a student worker when I saw that there was one who was not busy. When I told my mom about this, she all but declared the situation hopeless; my supervisor was not going to keep to any agreements, and I needed to leave in order to preserve my sanity. And when it came to my sanity, there was much to be worried about. Even before the night I banged my head against the wall, my mom had concerns about the impact my job was having on my mental health. In addition to sleeping all day and not grooming myself on the weekends, my mom noticed I was having memory lapses.

Frankly, at the risk of sounding facetious, I must confess to having no memory of having memory lapses. What I do remember is losing my Theory of Mind. My tendency to conflate my own anxieties about my self-worth with how others saw me was becoming magnified. In this case, it all centered on the word "prioritize," the word that I felt had been weaponized against me. To me, the word "prioritize" became equivalent to a car backfiring to a combat veteran, a non-threatening sound that put me immediately on a war footing. This innocuous word called to mind everything I'd been told was wrong with me my whole life. It was conflated with every lost jacket, misplaced document, and neglected-until-the-last-minute homework assignment. And, worst yet, the word "prioritize" reminded me that regardless of how much I might grow and improve, I was always just one mistake or misunderstanding away from being judged a complete failure.

So, when my mom one day, off-handedly, remarked, "oh, you do have trouble prioritizing," it hit me like a branding iron. We were on our way to Professor Gates' house for a party or reception, and we were running a little late. On the way, we had to make a quick stop, and instead of just getting out, taking care of the errand, and getting back in the car, I took the time to throw something in a nearby trash can. That's when my mom made the comment about me being unable to prioritize. I don't remember my immediate response; I think I was just stunned. I managed to keep myself together enough to not cause a scene at Professor Gates' house, though I did let my mom know, in a stern whisper when we were alone, just how much her words had wounded me.

My mother felt that I needed to take time off work, and the day after my contentious meeting with my supervisor, my union rep, and Human Resources was the last day I ever set foot in Lamont Library as an employee. I didn't quit; instead, I called the Benefits Office and inquired about how I would go about taking a medical leave. I was told there was no medical leave. What I needed to do was apply for short-term disability. Dr. Dinklage had retired about a year before I started working at Lamont, and my current therapist was a psychiatric nurse with expertise in Asperger's Syndrome acquired at the Yale Child Study Center. She felt, as my mom did, that I needed to take time off work, and she agreed to write a letter on my behalf.

Before writing the letter, however, my therapist needed to consult with her supervisor, a psychiatrist I had never actually met. This psychiatrist emphasized the importance of downplaying my disability and advised my therapist to focus on the conflict with my supervisor as causing my current "occupational stress." Ironically, downplaying my disability and emphasizing my "occupational stress" backfired—my claim was rejected because it "seems work-related." When I inquired about filing a Worker's Compensation claim, I was told that job stress cases are usually rejected by Harvard. I applied anyway, my claim was rejected, and I was told my only recourse was to appeal the decision to the Department of Industrial Accidents and appear before a judge. I later learned that cases in which a mental illness or disability is involved are almost impossible to win because there is a higher burden of proof placed on the plaintiff. When dealing with physical injury, the fact that you were hurt on the job is sufficient. In the case of mental injury, you must demonstrate that not only was the job the primary cause of your need for treatment but also that the injury was not the result of a bona fide personnel action.

My mother and I once visited a Worker's Compensation lawyer who offered an interesting perspective on why working might be difficult for people on the autism spectrum. After listening to my story, he said he needed to consult with a colleague, and while he was on the phone, he said something that really rang true. In trying to explain an autistic employee's difficulties, he said, "you know you, and I might have a shouting match and then go out for coffee after work. For someone with autism, that'd be too stressful." For someone who felt ill-equipped to deal with my case because, as he put it, he's a "broken bones guy," this lawyer perfectly encapsulated one of my major problems. Conflict has always been my Achilles Heel.

My mother encouraged me to get a lawyer who might have experience dealing with a cognitive disability. A few phone calls led me to the Mental Health Legal Advisors Committee, which operates under the auspices of the Supreme Judicial Court of Massachusetts. When I introduced myself to the senior attorney, Susan Fendell, and told her I was calling about something having to do with Harvard, she responded sarcastically, "Boy, they're doing such wonderful things over there." Fendell's first piece of advice was for me to get a copy of the short-term disability policy, a task that proved more difficult than I could ever have imagined. No one I asked, whether in Human

Resources or Benefits, seemed to know what I was talking about. I kept being given pamphlets and brochures or referred to websites that reiterated the information in the pamphlets and brochures. But no one was able to produce a copy of the actual policy.

Nonetheless, I submitted my appeal for short-term disability, which Fendell had urged me to do as soon as possible since short-term disability is only retroactive for one week. I wasn't surprised when my appeal was denied. What came as a complete shock was the personal attack leveled against my mom and me.

According to the denial letter, I never told anyone at Harvard about my autism until my supervisor denied me a vacation request. The letter also insinuated that my mother had somehow managed to get me illegally covered under her insurance before I became a Harvard employee. Included with the letter were writings from an expert on Asperger's Syndrome talking about how people with the condition can become college professors or computer programmers. My mother and I would spend hours gathering the documents needed to refute each of the denial letter's false claims.

Meanwhile, there was a back-and-forth between my lawyer, Susan Fendell, and Harvard's lawyer regarding what, if any, accommodations could be made to enable me to return to my job at Lamont. The opening salvo was Harvard's response to a list of accommodations my mom and I had left with Harvard's Disability Coordinator. My major ask was for concrete performance standards that I could follow, something Harvard's lawyer said was impossible given the nature of being a library assistant at Lamont.

According to Harvard's lawyer, my job was impossible to quantify. How did she know? She had consulted with my supervisor and learned just how fast-paced and ever-changing the Office of Technical Services was on any given day. In response to my suggestion of a lateral move to a position at Hilles Library, Lamont's undergraduate sister, I was informed that all jobs at Harvard were the same; complex, multi-layered, undefinable. What was quite clear, however, according to Harvard's counsel, was that I had had a great supervisor; she had been "kind and gentle" with me even though I was an impossible employee.

In fact, my performance and medical records clearly showed that the problem was not with my supervisor at all but with me; my autism rendered me incapable of handling the normal stresses of working at the Harvard College Library. I remember how my mom was struck by what Harvard was unintentionally saying.

By this time, we had been not only able to get a copy of the short-term disability policy but also the long-term disability policy. The latter defined a disability as one that prevented someone from doing a job others of similar age and educational background were currently engaged in as a means of "gainful employment." If what Harvard was saying was true, my mom realized, and my autism made me incapable of working in a library even though I had been trained as a librarian, wasn't Harvard, in essence, suggesting that I should be on long-term disability?

And who was I to insist that I was performing adequately? Paperwork and time management had never been my fortes, and one reason I wanted performance standards from my supervisor was that I honestly wanted to know if I was too slow. And did I have conflicts with my supervisor and some co-workers? Sure, but a lot of people did, yet were still able to go about their business and live their lives. Did my autism have something to do with why I found the clichés of office politics so overwhelmingly stressful and impossible to handle? So, in response to Harvard's missives, I agreed with my mom; I should apply for long-term disability.

Incidentally, while applying for long-term disability forced me to acknowledge the truth in some of the things being said about me, it also offered me the opportunity to directly address statements Harvard made that were not true. As part of the long-term disability application, my mom and I gathered all the documents necessary to refute the accusations made against both of us. We showed that contrary to the denial letter's claim that I never told anyone at Harvard about my autism, I had been seeing a therapist at Harvard's University Health Services for autism since I moved to Cambridge in 1997. Furthermore, we demonstrated that the denial letter's musings about how it was that I came to be covered by Harvard insurance before my employment was completely without foundation since the rules clearly stated my mom had every right to have me covered under her plan. My application for long-term disability was a large three-ring notebook containing some 30 years' worth of medical records, social security documentation, and other supplemental material.

Though hoping for the best, I was anticipating an automatic denial that would be followed by an appeal; that's what Fendell suggested would happen, and she was right. What I did not anticipate and found almost mortifying was the hearing in which I came face-to-face with the author of the letter containing all the falsehoods my mom and I had so painstakingly refuted. The letter this person had written so traumatized me that I saw her, perhaps unreasonably, as my arch enemy, my nemesis. I was appalled that she would have anything to do with my case.

At any rate, I was assured that though my perceived foe would be participating in the hearing, she wouldn't have a vote. I was so focused on her and the fact that, during the hearing, she did most, if not, all the talking, I missed a dynamic that seemed to be working in my favor. According to my mom, who accompanied me to the meeting along with Susan Fendell, some of the members of the Benefits Committee were visibly disturbed when they heard about my supervisor placing my desk so that my back was facing my co-workers. I probably would have missed it anyway, and, in any case, it didn't prevent my claim from being denied. When my mother and I appealed, my records were sent to an external reviewer. The external reviewer determined that my disability was serious enough to prevent me from working. Moreover, she also opined that I had been poorly served by a failure to recognize the severity of my condition.

So, persistence paid off. I won. Once again, David beat Goliath; another in a pattern of historical upsets that had it not repeated itself sometime in the 18th century, Harvard, the superior force I was up against, might still be a British university. In my euphoria, I could wax eloquent about the power of passivity. I could compare myself to boxer Mohammed Ali when he rope-a-doped George Forman or to the Russian general Marshal Kutuzov when he defeated Napoleon by methodically retreating and leading the French army into the depths of a Siberian winter. But those were by design. In truth, I was more like the salmon I once heard about on a trip to Alaska who, when set upon by an eagle, just kept swimming out to sea until the hungry bird who wouldn't or couldn't let go drowned. I had no strategy. I was just trying to survive.

And the way I survived was by falling on my sword. At least, that's how it felt. I was forced to openly embrace the most cutting criticisms regardless of how much it killed me. I had to admit that I was not the most efficient or organized worker and that I did get easily overwhelmed by the stress of having to juggle multiple responsibilities. I also had to explicitly acknowledge that my successes, as significant as they were, did not come without significant assistance from my mom and academic accommodations from my teachers. But there was a twist: instead of being a disgruntled (and disturbed) employee who concocted a disability to get time off work, I was a legitimate autistic who had tried their best but failed to get the help they needed. Where before there was antipathy, now there was sympathy.

Chapter Nine: The System

Two years later, Harvard contacted me to schedule a review of my disability status. The question under consideration was whether I was capable of gainful employment. Since leaving my job at Lamont, and especially since coming to terms with the resolution of my long-term disability claim, I had, for the most part, been on an even keel. The optimist in me could easily have forgotten how overwhelmed and stressed-out I became working at Lamont. The situation was analogous to what my primary care doctor warned me about my asthma when I once made the mistake of stating I was cured of the condition. No, my asthma was under control, my doctor reminded me, thanks to both my daily and rescue inhalers. However, if I became complacent and took the fact that I rarely, if ever, needed my rescue inhaler (even after engaging in vigorous exercise) as a sign that I no longer needed my daily one, the consequences could be disastrous.

The same was true with my ability to handle the world of work. I could write slogans for the Asperger's Association of New England's (AANE) annual appeal, offer my two cents at board meetings, and even run a small book club; but my activities, as much as they gave me a sense of purpose and importance, were nothing like holding down a full-time job. For one thing, everything I did, I did for free, which meant that the stakes were far lower and, my "employers" could just appreciate whatever I happened to produce. There's a world of difference between being an employee reporting to a supervisor and being a volunteer lending a helping hand. So, when the appointment was made for me to be evaluated by a Dr. Rater at McLean Hospital, I was a little concerned that my volunteer activities at AANE would be confused as actual employment. Still, no one could reasonably draw that conclusion, could they?

The trip to Dr. Rater's office was uneventful until we arrived at the main entrance to McLean Hospital. The Ride picked me up on time, and the driver knew where he was going. These were not small considerations. When I first got the Ride in 2002, the service was not always reliable. In the beginning, there was some confusion about whether, when making a reservation, I should ask to be picked up at a particular time or tell the agent what time I wanted to arrive at my destination. Even though I was always told to opt for the latter, the computer would sometimes generate a pick-up time that was identical to the one I had asked for. Then there was that misunderstanding that occurred when I took one of my first rides to Cambridge Health Alliance in Somerville. It had been raining, and the windows were all fogged up, so I didn't realize I was being driven to Somerville Hospital several miles out-of-the-way until it was too late. But by July 2006, when I was going to my evaluation with Rater, the Ride and I had long since figured out how to communicate where I was going and what time I needed to be there. There were certain routine places I went whose addresses were kept on file, and the times I was given were consistently sufficient to get me to my destination on time. My use of the Ride had broken it in like a stiff piece of leather that now fit like a comfortable shoe.

Problems arose when Mclean's main entrance turned out to simply be a gateway into a sprawling campus of red brick buildings, green pastures, white picket fences, and paved country roads. Usually, I would have found such an environment peaceful and inspiring, but now, trying to find the location of my appointment, this vast pastoral expanse could not have been more frustrating and crazy-making. After driving around for a few minutes in what seemed like out in the middle of nowhere, the driver finally went into one of the brick buildings to ask for directions. When I finally reached Dr. Rater's building, I was not relieved for now I had the problem of how the Ride was going to know where to pick me up to take me home. "Just call the dispatcher and tell him where you are," was the only advice the driver could give me.

Rater's building was a stylishly chiseled red brick structure that looked like it could have been a little clubhouse on a small liberal arts college campus. Walking into the building, I was greeted by a bulletin board covered with flyers which completed the college theme nicely. But there, the similarities ended. The rest of the interior made it quite clear that this was a hospital and nothing else, plain white walls with black trim along the baseboards, off-white flooring with no discernible pattern, and an interior design of stark lines but no color contrasts. Everything just kind of blended into a general sense of antiseptic austerity. I barely remember the receptionist who directed me to wait outside Rater's office.

I admit I was more than just a little anxious, so my memory of details is somewhat fuzzy. For instance, I remember what Dr. Rater looked like (a balding medium-sized man in his late thirties or early forties dressed in a light blue collared shirt and dark trousers), but I cannot remember anything about his office. In my mind's eye, I am unable to make out any pictures, plaques, or other office signatures. I don't even know if the computer on Rater's desk was a laptop or desktop. Sitting in front of Rater's desk, my attention was drawn to the window behind him and the partial view of McLean's campus.

As I remember it, the interview began the moment I took my seat.

"Why are you here?"

"This is my post-two-year long-term disability evaluation."

My simple answer to a simple question was, as my mother later reminded me, completely wrong. The Rater evaluation was not a two-year review even though I had been on Long-term Disability for two years. For some reason, back in 2004, the initial review and the two-year review were condensed. Indeed, the series of neuropsychological tests I had taken shortly after initially being placed on Long-term Disability was my post-24-month review. My visit with Rater was simply Harvard exercising its right to periodically check up on the status of my disability.

Rater continued with his preliminaries.

"Are you married?"

"No."

"Do you have a girlfriend?"

"No."

"Do you have any children?"

"No."

There was an opportunity for small talk when Rater told me that he knew one of my previous psychiatrists, Dr. Mohatt, who Rater informed me, was now living somewhere in the south. I could have confided in Rater that Mohatt became a developmental milestone for me when soon after my thirtieth birthday, I learned that he was still twenty-nine. I could have joked, "you know you're getting old when you're older than your doctor." But I hesitated too long, and the moment passed.

The longest exchange occurred when Rater wanted me to account for my daily activities. He wanted a detailed accounting of when I woke up in the morning, what I did from that time until lunch; what I did from lunch until dinner; and what time I went to bed. I struggled with trying to fit the previous two years of my life into Rater's strict parameters because I didn't follow a conventional routine. I went to bed very late at night and rarely woke up in the morning unless absolutely necessary; I also did not have a set lunch, dinner, or bedtime. When I think about it, much of my eclectic schedule can be traced directly back to my disability.

Growing up, I had a lot of trouble in school. My mother and I would stay up all through the night, sometimes with neither of us getting any sleep, while she helped me complete my homework assignments or work through problems I was having with teachers or classmates. This pattern continued through my college and graduate school years and even manifested itself while I was working at Lamont.

Maybe I could have explained all this to Rater, but that wouldn't have absolved me from having to meticulously account for my time. I tried to give Rater a general sense of my schedule by listing my weekly therapy appointments, a writing class I was taking, and my participation in AANE, but he wanted me to be more specific.

"What activities do you engage in with AANE?"

"I participate in a weekly discussion group with other adults on the Autism Spectrum. I also volunteer for the organization by serving on the Board of Directors and attending monthly board meetings, facilitating a book club, and writing a slogan for the annual appeal."

"What does facilitating the book club entail?"

"I choose the books and lead the discussion."

"How many people are in the book club?"

"There are no regular members. Only one or two people show up on a consistent basis."

"What type of books do you read?"

"We focus on books having to do with autism and Asperger's syndrome."

"I guess that's the point, isn't it?" Rater commented while typing into his computer.

Throughout the interview, Rater was always typing on his computer. As I said, I didn't register whether it was a laptop or a desktop, but the computer on his desk was placed off to the side, thus allowing Rater to maintain a modicum of eye contact with me while his hands remained prone in the typing position. I only remember one instance in which Rater relaxed his typist's pose and focused directly on me. I was explaining how my writing class at the Cambridge Adult Center was helping me to overcome my writer's block by encouraging me to write from my immediate thoughts when Rater interrupted me, "Hey, it's been ten years—where's the book?" Where was the book? It was dispersed amid a flurry of discarded false starts and a few short, disembodied descriptions, the product of my difficulties writing at length and my tendency towards self-censorship and premature editing. I don't remember how much of this I explained to Rater. I only remember my embarrassment at his accusatory tone and my relief when his attention returned to his typing.

I was momentarily relieved when the interview was finally over, but that sense of relief was only temporary. While I was on the phone with the Ride dispatcher trying to find my way back to McLean's entrance, my ambient thoughts were an internal debate about how much I may or may not have just screwed up. I shouldn't have said all that stuff about AANE, but I couldn't just sit there in silence. AANE had taken up a lot of my time in the previous two years, and frankly, I felt good about my status as an important member of the autism community. Did I wear too much of this pride on my sleeve? Did I give Rater reason to believe that I was somehow employed by AANE? No, I know I made it clear that I was a volunteer. But still, could writing slogans and running a book club be taken to be "gainful activity" as defined in the long-term disability rules?

By the time I met my ride at the entrance to McLean Hospital, I was thoroughly rattled. I kept replaying the interview over and over again, asking myself the same questions. Did I say too much? Did I say too little? Should I have phrased things differently? Did I just dispose of my only source of income? Later that night, I was watching a movie in which a defendant was being cross-examined by a particularly aggressive prosecutor. The man on the stand was reduced to almost incoherent mumbling while his interrogator hovered over him, pointing an accusatory finger and firing off questions as fast as sentences could fly. That scene encapsulated for me how I felt about my interview with Rater.

When I received Rater's report sometime later, I learned that everything I had feared had come to pass. Rater did interpret my activities with AANE as evidence that I was capable of gainful employment. He quoted an autism website that stated people with Asperger's Syndrome could work in the right environment. What Rater did not mention, but no doubt read, was this same website's list of luminaries like Albert Einstein, Emily Dickinson, and Isaac Newton, among a plethora of others, who had been posthumously placed on the Autism Spectrum.

When I was first diagnosed autistic, I used to love to look for autistic tendencies not only in historical figures but also in celebrities and people I knew. I figured autism had probably always existed, and I couldn't be the only autistic the experts missed. I also hoped that a wide recognition of the autistic tendencies in cultural icons would make my own autism more palatable to society.

Time taught me that I couldn't have been more misguided. Remote diagnosis did seem to catch on as a trend, but it didn't necessarily translate into greater acceptance or respect. In fact, as my mother often worried would happen, the reframing of autism as a unique type of ability was doing more harm than good. We only had to look to Harvard's skepticism regarding my own disability to illustrate her point.

After Rater's report led to me being thrown off Long-term Disability, and my mother and I appealed the decision, an appointment was set up for me to be evaluated by a Dr. Clayman, a psychologist who specialized in malingering. To my surprise, I felt at ease during my evaluation with Clayman. The question-and-answer portion of the evaluation lulled me into a sense of almost serenity; I felt comfortable speaking with a grandfatherly man who, unlike Rater, seemed genuinely interested in what I had to say. By the time Clayman left me alone to take the Minnesota Multiphasic Personality Inventory, I was completely relaxed—the fact that I knew that I could take a break at any point did much to put me in a mellow mood.

However, I still had concerns about the evaluation. The skills portion of Clayman's exam was minimal compared to the battery of tests administered to me back in 2004. For instance, Clayman assessed my math ability by asking me how much change I should get back if something costs $10.50, and I gave the clerk $18. My reading ability was measured by having me recite a shortlist of words that never got more complicated than what any college-educated, native speaker of English would know. And my ability to identify an object placed in my hand while my eyes were closed was also tested. Was this a trap? Was the bar being set deliberately low so I could easily clear it?

My suspicions of Clayman were matched by his suspicions of me. One thing he found odd and felt compelled to ask me about was why I knew so many psychological terms. When I explained to him that one of my majors in college had been psychology, I thought the matter was settled. However, Clayman still noted my apparent knowledge of psychology as a curious fact in his final report. What was he implying? One thing he made abundantly clear, though, was his opinion that I was perfectly capable of working because of my "good language skills."

Clayman was so confident in his assessment of me that he took it upon himself to defy the written record. Indeed, Clayman conceded that I tested more like a person with high-functioning autism than Asperger's syndrome; however, he made the determination that I had Asperger's syndrome. Dr. Clayman's report led to a denial of my appeal, which my mom and I subsequently appealed. Next to come were affidavits from me, my mom, and my therapist; Clayman's response to said affidavits; and another hearing with the Benefits Committee in which I was accompanied by my mom and Susan Fendell. Around this time, Harvard's disability benefits system was outsourced to a private company called Standard Insurance. A review of my case by a claims representative resulted in a reinstatement of my Long-term Disability, which I have been receiving ever since with no drama.

Even though I derived a sense of purpose from my volunteer work, I still felt like there was something missing in my life. But autism was not my only obstacle to getting a job. More significant, especially in the library world, was my lack of professional experience. Almost every job listing, even for entry-level positions, required at least two years of professional experience, a conundrum that seemed unsolvable, and bordered on the tautological; to get a job, I needed work experience which I could only accumulate by working at a job.

Finally, this Gordian knot was cut by Peter Obuchan, the library director at Newbury College in Brookline just outside of Boston, who hired me as a part-time reference librarian despite my lack of professional experience. A very unassuming middle-aged man who wore eyeglasses and whose dress tended towards business casual, Peter Obuchan would never strike one as harboring avant-garde or radical views. However, at least in the world of library hiring, he was a bit of a renegade. When Obuchon hired me, he did so, as I said, despite my lack of professional experience, a requirement he told me he considered both unreasonable and unnecessary.

The slow-paced, single-task focus of my job at Newbery College was the exact opposite of the fast-paced, frenetic multi-tasking medley of my job at Lamont. My only responsibility at Newbury College was to man the reference desk for a few hours every Sunday. The traffic was light, and I basically worked alone; my tasks were routine and included opening and closing the library and helping the few patrons who came to find the information they were looking for. The job was like a work-study position I had during my last year at Macalester in which I manned the computer stations in the college library in the evenings. Unfortunately, the fact that I worked on my own backfired when my supervisor declined to write a letter of recommendation for me on the grounds that she had never actually seen me work.

In order to prevent this history from repeating itself, my mom suggested that I ask Peter if there was anything I could work on that would lead to a finished product. Per my request, I was asked to compile lists of online resources to be placed on the library's home page. There were other opportunities for me to show my work, like when I led a group of students accompanied by their professor through an introduction to library resources. Another time, every cooking major in the college, it seemed, descended on the library in order to complete a big project. I welcomed the break from the routine offered by teaching the class and the challenge posed by the aspiring chefs, a reaction I attributed to a relaxed state of mind brought on by the usual quiet and serenity of my working environment.

Unfortunately, the job at Newbury was only temporary. The Sunday traffic was too light to justify the continuation of having a reference librarian on-hand even if only part-time; and though Peter was willing to write a recommendation for me, the eight months of experience I accumulated at Newbury College was not enough to satisfy those for whom only the most extensive professional experience, even for an entry-level position, was acceptable.

While my future was in flux, my mother, considering a career move from teaching to administration, was pursuing a master's at the Harvard Graduate School of Education. That's when she took the class in social scientific portraiture and interviewed me, leading to our joint presentations and our decision to write a book together.

Sitting for my mother's portrait got me back into the spirit of telling my own story. I really enjoyed being interviewed by my mom. I relished the opportunity to express myself on a variety of topics, and I appreciated seeing a lot of what I had to say appearing in print. However, my mom's portrait was not a puff piece. The portraitist is supposed to be generous but honest, and my mom's lens didn't always capture me in the best light. And that was perhaps one of the most powerful aspects of being portrayed by my mom; it didn't bother me when I came off looking less than noble, heroic, or even competent. Absent was my usual defensiveness. Instead of being offended or feeling maligned, I felt validated, even empowered. I didn't even care when my mom recorded a day in which I stumbled more than I strutted.

It was my mother's birthday, and I was to meet her after one of her classes so that we could walk over to the Harvard Faculty Club for dinner. I was elegantly dressed in a collared shirt, sports jacket, and slacks; unfortunately, I also had a case of red eye since, for some reason, I miscalculated and wound up opening my eyes too soon while washing my hair in the shower. Then there were the flowers I brought my mother. It was still cold even though it was April, and my mother had made an off-hand comment about the risk of flowers freezing. On my way to meet my mother, I came across a vendor in Harvard Square selling dried-out flowers that I realized certainly wouldn't freeze. Dried flowers—wasn't I being clever? My mom was not impressed. However, she also was not upset; she just chalked up the whole episode to the difficulty I've always had in buying her gifts.

My greatest hit of the evening occurred when my mother and I just happened to run into Sara Lawrence-Lightfoot, my mother's portraitist professor, at the Faculty Club right before sitting down for our meal. Actually, I was already seated chomping on the bread. My mother was talking to the receptionist about her membership, and on her way back to the table, she brought Professor Lawrence-Lightfoot, who wanted to meet me based on an early draft of my mother's portrait. As my mother described it, I managed to smile while pushing the bread to the side of my mouth, and I shook Professor Lawrence-Lightfoot's hand without standing up. My mother didn't hold it against me (nor, as it turned out, did Lawrence-Lightfoot, who later remarked, "hey, we surprised him") but saw it as a teaching moment to remind me about the manners I had temporarily neglected.

What struck me most about the whole affair was that I didn't care about the fact that my mother had recorded for posterity things I could easily have argued were anomalies. Indeed, I don't usually get shampoo in my eyes when I shower; I have managed to buy my mom sensible, even nice, presents; I'm certainly not in the habit of stuffing food in my mouth; and even though I consider myself a feminist, I still value being a gentleman. But what my mother said about me that day was true, and the way she framed it humanized me for the reader while offering broader lessons about autism. My mother even managed to portray one of my outbursts sympathetically. After quoting from something I wrote about the incident, my mother reflected upon the fraught nature of my struggle to reconcile the conflicting views I held of myself. In her capable hands, I didn't come off as either a monster or a monstrosity.

I was reminded of something I read in the slave narrative Incidents in the Life of a Slave Girl, Written by Herself by Harriet Jacobs. In her book, Jacobs revealed things about herself of which she was greatly ashamed in order to shed light on a little talked about aspect of slavery. To a modern audience, Jacob's confession that the unwanted sexual advances of her lecherous master led her into a romantic relationship with another white man might seem minor, but to her and her 19th-century reader, Jacob's behavior was potentially scandalous. Similarly, I realized that if my story was going to be of any use, I, too, needed to be willing to discuss things that I might find disturbing but were, nonetheless, instructive.

Chapter Ten:
Work, Interrupted

Before writing and presenting together, my mom and I had already started reading together. During my terrible teens, my mother, unbeknownst to me, would creatively visualize a peaceful scene of the two of us sitting side-by-side on a couch reading. Fast-forward a little over a decade, and that imagined scene became a routine reality. My mom and I would often find ourselves sitting on opposite ends of our couch reading, and, though we were usually reading different types of books, we'd share passages or plot lines that were of mutual interest. "Hey, mom, this sounds like what we've been talking about." "Gyasi, this is just like what I was saying the other day."

I don't know exactly what happened; all I can say is that growing up in a house of books and being raised by a mother who loved to read finally became a part of me. It's not that I ever had anything against reading, and I enjoyed the books I did read, but reading just wasn't an activity I gravitated to for pleasure. Then, while I was working at Lamont, I'd lose myself during breaks in the books displayed on the New York Times Bestseller shelf. Ready access to this shelf became one of the few benefits I felt remained from my job working in the library. My relationship with books began to change; instead of just admiring the cover and appreciating what a book represented (as I often did with the books in my mom's library), I found myself wanting to dive into them and extract their treasures for myself. Reading became a passion.

But, of course, the flip side of reading is writing. If writers didn't write, there'd be nothing to read. Now that I had become an avid consumer of words, my mother wanted to help me become a creator. And, here, too, the tumblers finally clicked into place. My mother had me enroll in a writing class at the Cambridge Center for Adult Education called "Memories, Stories, and Reflection," a class that demonstrated the truth of something my mom had been trying to tell me for years; writing is thinking on paper. "Writing is thinking on paper" was an adage with my mom and something she'd often repeat to her students and to me. I loved the way it sounded, I wanted to believe it, but I just couldn't feel it. All I could see was the huge gap between the free-floating thoughts bouncing around in my brain and the organized, stylized prose I hoped to produce on the page.

The writing class at the Cambridge Center for Adult Education worked on the powerful principle of prompts. Meeting once a week, each class began with five minutes of writing in response to something the teacher would throw out; a word, an image, any mental object, or a collection of objects from which our minds could draw associations and make connections. This process really loosened me up. There's an old joke about writers getting all formal when they sit down to write as though they've suddenly dawned a tuxedo before putting pen to paper. Well, during the five-minute sessions, I started to loosen my tie, roll up my sleeves, and kick my feet up on the desk.

I recorded the first thing that came to mind, and I was often pleased with the result. Equally important, so were my classmates. At the end of class, we'd be given a prompt to take home with us and use to create a longer piece, maybe 3-5 pages, over the course of the week. At the end of the semester, we'd select from what we'd written what pieces we'd like published in a bound booklet printed at a local Kinko's. I took the class for a few semesters, and much of what I wrote had little to do with my memoirs. However, through the process of focused freewriting, I began to see the reciprocity between thinking and writing. I could feel how my attempts to make sense of what was in my head influenced what appeared on the page and visa-versa. My mom was right! Writing is thinking on paper.

Plus, as my thinking became less rigid, I was able to take what I wrote in one context and apply it to another. As time went on, I became flexible enough to not only make the class prompts relevant to my memoirs but also to rework my desperate memories, stories and reflections into my larger narrative. And my life story would be part of the still bigger picture of my mom's portrait offering the world a couple of dual perspectives, mother and son, autistic and non-autistic. We'd always been a team. We'd now be writing partners. The way forward couldn't have been clearer.

Things become fuzzy when I try to pinpoint the first sign that there was something wrong with my mom. Was it the persistent pain in her side? Or was it the build-up of fluid in her lungs? Both symptoms had perfectly benign explanations; my mom had strained herself when we both tried to move a heavy piece of furniture, and she was recovering from a cold. It's a bit of a blur, but I remember an appointment with a radiologist, my mother having fluid drained from her lungs, and that fateful phone call during which my mother turned to me and said, "it's lung cancer." How did they know? Cancer cells were found in the fluid taken from my mother's lungs.

Next to come was an appointment with an oncologist at Lahey Hospital, who estimated that my mom had six months to a year to live, but there was hope. Depending on the genetic make-up of the cancer, targeted therapy might be an option. Even when cancer's genes failed to match any available medications, there was chemotherapy. Meanwhile, my mom was assigned a team that included a nurse navigator and social worker; an electronic system to measure my mom's vital signs was set up in our apartment; and we got periodic home visits from nurses.

I don't remember having much of a reaction to the news that my mom only had six months to a year to live, though my mom told me my face went completely white. What stands out to me the most is my mom's reaction; she turned to me, placed her hand on my back, and said, "Are you okay?" It was the perfect portrait of a selfless mother. My mom might also have wondered, "Will you be okay?" a question asked by many parents of disabled children when they are forced to confront their own mortality. The issue was put most succinctly in the title of a presentation delivered at the 2017 Autism Society of America Conference; "Developing a Housing Strategy: Because Mom and Dad Living Forever isn't a Plan."

My mom's strategy was to plan for the best but prepare for the worst. In addition to doing research on cancer and clinical trials, my mom had me apply to the Bedford Housing Authority. We also met with someone from the Boston Center for Independent Living and attended a special presentation on estate planning at the Bedford Council on Aging. Unfortunately, an appointment we made with someone at the Lurie Center for Autism who was knowledgeable about guardianship had to be canceled because my mom was in too much pain. When my mom wasn't having breathing problems because of the build-up of fluid in her lungs, she was almost immobilized by excruciating pain. As much as we wanted to plan for the future, we were forced to spend most of our time coping with the present.

The major issue was the unrelenting pain. My mom told me that the pain was what disturbed her most about cancer, not the possibility of death or the items left unchecked on her bucket list, but the pain. There was the nerve pain and the breakthrough pain, and the calculated administration of OxyContin and Oxycodone to handle both. There was my mom's negative reaction to morphine, some success with fentanyl patches, and finally, what seemed to be the Goldilocks solution: Dilaudid. But then my mom had difficulty swallowing. At first, it was thought that there was just a netting of cells in her throat; further tests revealed that it was part of the cancer.

The cancer was growing fast; it was so aggressive it broke one of my mom's ribs. After two courses of chemotherapy at Lahey proved ineffective, there was talk of hospice, but my mom and I were not ready to give up. Through our own research, we had learned about the promise of clinical trials, particularly those that combined traditional chemotherapy with immunotherapy. By stimulating the immune system to fight cancer cells, immunotherapy showed great potential; it had already been approved by the FDA as a treatment for certain cancers and was being actively investigated for others. Ironically, my mom first heard about clinical trials for cancer drugs while we were both participating in a focus group about clinical trials for autism drugs.

It was a trip that marked our transition from co-writing a book on autism to working together to fight cancer; my mom and I went to New York where we were put up in a hotel by a drug company conducting market research on what would make families impacted by autism willing to participate in clinical trials. We were broken into two groups: adults on the Autism Spectrum and the parents and caregivers of autistic adults. In my mom's group, one of the other mothers talked about her experience participating in a life-saving clinical trial when she had a cancer scare a few years earlier. My mother brought this nugget of knowledge back from our New York trip along with a cold that led to the fluid being drained from her lungs and the discovery of the cancer.

So, when the chemotherapy didn't work and while my mom was still corresponding with different cancer organizations about available clinical trials, she asked me to reach out to my psychiatrist, Dr.

Christopher McDougle, the director of the Lurie Center for Autism, a satellite of Massachusetts General Hospital (MGH). Was Dr. McDougle aware of any clinical trials happening at MGH? It turned out he was, and the name he gave matched a recommendation we had received from another source: Dr. Justin Gainor. My mother was deemed eligible for Dr. Gainor's trial and was subsequently enrolled. She would be receiving both traditional chemotherapy and immunotherapy. There was now new hope. As Dr. Gainor put it, "immunotherapy doesn't work often, but when it does, it works really well."

Along with the shift in focus from autism to cancer came a role reversal; my mom was now the patient, and I was the closest family member able to provide support. This forced me to see the world in a completely different way. I could no longer depend on my mom for everything; I needed to become more self-reliant. My mom had already been pushing me towards greater independence—coping with her cancer just accelerated the process. It was a Rites of Passage. As time went on, I felt more comfortable handing things on my own.

In addition to the bi-weekly trips to MGH for my mom's infusions and the periodic visits from home care nurses, there were other ways in which my mother's condition altered our daily routine. We had always shopped together, for instance, but now I had to push her in the hybrid wheelchair shopping carts in the supermarket. And, we had always cooked together, but now I was taking on more of the food prep and, as my mom's dietary needs and appetite changed, I was making her milkshakes and running to the local CVS to pick up applesauce.

My needs were still considered important, but most appropriately, in the context of how they might impact my ability to be there for my mom. For instance, during two of my mom's hospitalizations (there would be three during the course of her illness), I was allowed to stay in the room with her since I didn't drive. The one time I couldn't stay with my mom because she had a roommate, my cab fare back home was covered by MGH for the first night; my subsequent trips between Boston and Bedford were handled, of course, by The Ride. My ability to take care of my mom became a significant consideration when the chemo/immunotherapy combo failed to stop the cancer's spread, and it was time to talk seriously about hospice.

A decision had to be made. Could a hospital bed be set up in our apartment so that my mom could stay home, or did we have to find a facility that could either accommodate the both of us and/or was in a town covered by The Ride? The hospital-bed-in-apartment idea was discarded almost immediately by the determination that my mom needed 24-hour supervision by a staff of skilled nurses. Between a place in a town covered by The Ride and a nursing home that could house the two of us, my mom preferred the latter. As it happened, my mom's final placement offered us both; Walden Rehab was in Concord (right next door to Bedford), and my mom was given a double room so that I could be her roommate.

Unfortunately, my mom's condition quickly deteriorated within a couple of weeks of entering Walden Rehab. At first, my mom was fully alert and able to talk, and it looked like we might even be able to do some future planning. I'd already brought some things from the apartment based on a list we'd drawn up together. The plan was for me to go back and collect some papers; we might even be able to get back to our book. But then everything changed. While she remained conscious, my mom slipped into what could best be described as a state of semi-sedation. Part of it was the heavy medication she was on to manage the pain and agitation, but also, her system was shutting down. I was told that hearing was the last sense to go, so I should just keep talking to her, and I did though she rarely answered back. The only plans I was being asked to make now were choosing a funeral home and deciding between burial and cremation.

By this time, I was not dealing with this on my own but with the help of a coterie of family and friends. When my mom was first diagnosed in March of 2017, we kept things on a strictly need-to-know basis. My mom didn't want to broadcast that she had cancer because she feared being written off as already dead, and she didn't want to burden people with information they could do nothing about. But as my mom's condition worsened, more and more people needed to be informed until, by the time my mom wound up at Walden in August, almost everyone we knew was in the know. While at Walden, my mom and I received a lot of emotional support. Friends and family sent flowers, posted well wishes on my Facebook page, made phone calls, and a few even managed to visit.

My mom and I also received practical support. My Aunt Roslyn came up from New York and stayed in our apartment the whole time we were at Walden, and my Aunt Juanita flew in from California and helped me run some errands. Juanita also took over the financial planning my mother hadn't had an opportunity to complete. In addition to the agency of my aunts, I also benefited from a network of associations through my various community activities, six degrees of separation connecting me to a variety of civic organizations in Bedford and autism organizations throughout Massachusetts. I would come to rely on this network extensively when it came time for me to move.

My mom and I were alone when she passed away on September 13, 2017. She was having trouble breathing—at least, that's what I thought was going on. A few days earlier, a nurse's aide suggested that my mom needed some extra oxygen, but further testing showed her oxygen saturation levels to be normal. Thinking that my mom's oxygen saturation levels had fallen (something that had occurred earlier during the course of her illness), I went to the nurse's station for assistance. On my own deathbed, I imagine I'll still be pondering how I managed to misread all the signs.

"She should just let go," is all the nurse's aide who accompanied me back to the room said before leaving. I remember thinking, "so my mom's okay, she's not having breathing problems—maybe she'll just fall asleep." Then, a few moments later, all noise coming from my mom ceased. It was like a generator had been running at a low rumble, and someone had suddenly pulled the plug. So that noise my mom was making wasn't labored breathing—it must have been the death rattle. I returned to the nurse's station only to have confirmed what I already knew. My mother was gone.

Soon after my grandfather's sudden death in 2001, my mom, in a moment of reflection, said to me, "well, he knew you were doing okay. He knew you'd graduated from Macalester College and had a library degree from Simmons." She didn't mention my job at Harvard, though my grandfather took great pride in that, and, incidentally, he didn't know about the trouble I was having at Lamont. What did my mom see of me before she passed away? According to the nursing staff at Walden, my mom had raised an exemplary son, a message they'd often repeat in her presence. But was my mom really hearing this, and did she agree that my just being there was something special?

One impression I left with my mom had to do with my future living arrangements, and it was wrong, but in a good way; the reality turned out to be better. When I'd first applied to the Bedford Housing Authority in June, I'd been placed on an 8-10 year waiting list. In August, I got a letter from the Bedford Housing Authority with the welcome news that I'd made it to the top of the list. All that was needed from me were some bank statements, a birth certificate, and proof of my income from social security and long-term disability. My mom and I would have loved for me to stay in Avalon at Bedford Center, the complex we'd lived in ever since moving to Bedford from Cambridge in 2008; however, I'd already found out that there was actually an income limit to qualify for Avalon's affordable housing, and my income was too low. I'd also been told that there was a waiting list and, no, being an Avalon resident would not move me up in the line.

But I wasn't dismayed. I liked the apartment the Bedford Housing Authority showed me. It was small, but it had a nice look with hardwood floors and an enclosed balcony. Yes, the Bedford Housing Authority's Ashby Place was a bit further from the center of town than Avalon, but I figured I could use the exercise. All this I shared with my mom with the level of excitement you might expect if I were announcing I'd just made a down payment on a new house. It was my way of letting her know that I was going to be okay. And I was perfectly ready to start my new life in another section of Bedford. But my mom's death inspired Avalon at Bedford Center to evaluate my situation with compassion and empathy. An affordable housing, one-bedroom apartment was held aside for me, and I was encouraged to submit an application.

When my income fell short of the minimum required, I was still approved with the stipulation that someone could provide me with financial assistance if necessary, which Juanita agreed to do. So, when I had the choice between the one-bedroom at Ashby Place and the one-bedroom at Avalon, I chose the latter. The apartment at Avalon was bigger, which would make the already daunting task of downsizing from a two-bedroom, three-bathroom townhouse with a garage far easier. And I felt most at home in the Avalon at Bedford Center community and surrounding neighborhood.

- - -

My mother was finally getting her due. A tribute to her as a film scholar appeared in the New York Amsterdam News thanks, in part, to her association with the writer Ishmael Reed. My mom had worked for Ishmael Reed while she was a student at Berkeley, and they had remained friends. Over the years, Ishmael Reed had served as a role model for me as well as a source of encouragement like when he published my poems in his <u>Konch Image</u> magazine. Now, he was helping me honor my mother's legacy.

Certainly, my mother had received acknowledgment for her accomplishments in the past; but for the most part, she always struck me as an unsung hero. My mother had the type of intelligence that seemed to know no bounds; she wasn't just great at certain things; she had the ability to excel at almost anything. However, she devoted much of her talent and energy to raising and nurturing me. Yet, even with the obstacles inherent in being a single parent to a disabled child, my mom still managed to earn a Ph.D. in English from UCLA (she was the first black woman to do so), make significant contributions to scholarship in more than one field, design innovative courses that transformed students' lives and organize academic conferences that fostered community while celebrating the life of the mind.

I was glad to be able to write an obituary that chronicled my mother's achievements and a eulogy that commemorated her character. The eulogy was well-received, with the officiating pastor even going so far as to say it was the best she had ever read. For me, writing the eulogy was particularly poignant since my mom had helped me write the one I delivered at my grandmother's funeral almost a decade earlier. A few days after my mother's funeral, I had a dream in which my mom and I were in my grandparents' old apartment, an apartment that had been a part of the family from 1960 until my grandmother's death in 2009. After announcing with a flourish, "Mom, you are about to become the first person in history to hear their own eulogy," I read it pretty much as I had at the funeral until, when I got to the last sentence, I broke down and cried.

Afterword

O n April 9, 2019, what would have been my mother's 70th birthday, I was at a Disability Policy Seminar in Washington, D.C, preparing to visit with legislators the next day on Capitol Hill. I was traveling with a group of people I'd gotten to know well over the previous year as a Fellow in the LEND Program at Boston Children's Hospital. The purpose of LEND, which stands for Leadership Education in Neurodevelopmental and Related Disabilities, is to provide expert treatment and care to infants, children, and adolescents with disabilities while also preparing future professionals for leadership roles in maternal and child health. There are 52 LEND Programs covering all 50 states and 3 US territories: each one connected with a university hospital or medical center. There are two LENDs in Massachusetts—one at the Eunice Kennedy Shriver Center at UMass Medical School and the other at Boston Children's Hospital. Being a LEND Fellow exposed me to a world I never knew existed.

Like with LEND Programs across the country, my classmates came from a variety of academic disciplines and walks-of-life; there were graduate students, career professionals, people with disabilities, and family members of people with disabilities, representing such fields as law, medicine, psychology, audiology, as well as physical and occupational therapy. The Disability Policy Seminar and Capitol Hill visits were the capstones to a year of attending weekly lectures, collaborating on group projects, and engaging in fieldwork. My mother could have been a LEND Fellow, and she would have fit in perfectly with the other Fellows with disabled family members—particularly the graduate students with autistic children.

And there would have been nothing better than spending her 70th birthday in Washington, DC. It being the last night of the conference, the LEND faculty treated the Fellows to dinner at the Capitol Hill Brewing Company, and a group of us later sang Karaoke at the Wok & Roll Restaurant. My mom would have loved it. The next day she would have had much to contribute as we made the rounds to different congressional offices on Capitol Hill.

I was introduced to LEND by Maura Sullivan, one of the autism moms who rallied around me as my mother's condition worsened and after she passed away. It began with Maura telling me about an autism conference that might have had my mother turning in her urn. There was nothing wrong with the conference itself—in fact, it was perfect. The problem was the location and my poor sense of direction. The conference was called "Targeting Autism: Helping Libraries Serve Neurodiverse Communities," and it was being held at the Illinois State Library in Springfield, IL. While my mother would have loved the fact that I was speaking on a panel of autistic librarians, she would have been appalled at the concept of me negotiating a connecting flight through Dallas, TX, by myself in order to get to the conference. I might have been concerned too, had it not been for the fact that, by this point, I'd crossed so many comfort zones I was pretty much up for anything.

My travel to and from Springfield went off without a hitch, and I had a great time at the conference. When I returned, there was an e-mail from Maura waiting for me telling me about the LEND Program at Boston Children's Hospital. The LEND Program was looking for someone with a disability (also known as a self-advocate) to join the 2018-19 class, and Maura felt that I should apply. As it would turn out, there would be two self-advocates in my cohort; I and a woman named Donna Jay, a prominent member of a statewide self-advocacy organization called Mass Advocates Standing Strong. Donna was in her mid to late 50s, and I was in my mid-40s, making us two of the oldest people in the class. Most of the other students were in their mid to late 20s and early 30s, meaning that at the time of my diagnosis, many of them were small children—some hadn't even been born yet. Now, here we all were interacting as peers.

But despite my years of experience with autism, LEND still had much to teach me about disability. One takeaway was the history of advocacy going back decades. Long before I ever questioned autism discourse, there were many people successfully challenging the status quo leaving a legacy of legislative and regulatory achievements. The following are just some of the policy changes that have occurred during my own lifetime:

- 1973 – Rehabilitation Act prohibits programs receiving federal funds from discriminating based on disability.
- 1975 - Education for All Handicapped Children Act (later renamed IDEA for Individuals with Disabilities Education Act) mandates a free and appropriate public education for all disabled children.
- 1990 - Americans with Disabilities Act bans discrimination against disabled people in employment as well as in public accommodations and services.
- 1999 - Supreme Court Olmstead Decision declares the unjustified segregation of the disabled as discrimination in violation of Title II of the Americans with Disabilities Act.
- 2014 - Center for Medicare and Medicaid Services Final Rule requires that federal funds for Home and Community-Based Services be used only in the most integrated setting.

The above landmarks are part of a paradigm shift away from a medical model of disability which focuses on the defects within the individual towards a social model that strives to eliminate barriers within society. This trend has had a significant impact on my life. Indeed, the Individuals with Disabilities Education Act authorized my special education classes in grade school, and the Americans with Disabilities Act granted me the right to academic accommodations in college and grad school. But, more broadly, the social model of disability created a climate of acceptance and inclusion, the type of climate that welcomed me into the LEND Program, where I gained a deeper understanding of the systems set up to support me.

LEND also taught me something about myself. The class was asked to complete the Myers-Briggs Personality Inventory in preparation for a session explaining the meaning behind the four sets of letters. Since I had already taken the Myers-Briggs a few years earlier, I didn't have to repeat it. I knew my type; I was an INTJ. At least, that's what I thought. As the facilitator went through the first three sets of letters, everything matched. I was an "I" for introvert instead of an "E" for extrovert; an "N" for intuitive as opposed to an "S" for sensing; and a "T" for thinking, not an "F" for feeling. When we got to the last set of letters, "J" for judging and "P" for perceiving, there was a glitch. I identified with the description of the "J," the organized list-maker, but when I heard that the "P" was easily distracted and often lost in meandering streams of consciousness, I recognized myself immediately. How could this be? I was an INTJ, not an INTP. Of Course, the Myers-Briggs could simply have been wrong, but how could I account for the first three letters being so spot on? When I looked closer at my earlier results, I discovered something interesting; whereas my "I," "N," and "T" registered as "Clear" or "Very Clear," my "J" was only "Slight."

Upon further reflection, it all made sense. I was raised by a "J." My mother was the consummate planner who always stressed the importance of making lists and being organized. Indeed, looking back, I can see that one of the forces she was up against was my inclination towards disorganization. Now, I was inclined to wonder if the "P" in my personality was a curse. But what if it wasn't all bad? What if it was my wandering mind that enabled me to recognize connections between disparate things? Maybe it's what led me to a double major in English and psychology or what attracted me to the interdisciplinary nature of the LEND Program. Should I force myself to be a "J," or could I make "P" work for me? Maybe I could benefit from having aspects of both.

The highlight of the LEND Program was the trip to Washington D.C. to meet with members of the Massachusetts delegation: our nine representatives and two senators. Leading up to the Hill visits would be the Disability Policy Seminary, a 3-day conference during which we would meet and mingle with LEND Fellows from across the country. On the day of the Hill visits, we would be divided into groups of 4 or 5 and given a schedule before being sent off to the offices of 2 or 3 representatives and one of the senators. More likely than not, we would be meeting with a congressional aid, and depending on space availability, the meeting could take place in an enclosed waiting area, a small conference room, or a well-appointed office. After a team leader introduced our group, each of us would spend a minute or two talking about pieces of legislation that held personal significance for us.

And the personal significance was integral to how we would capture the imagination of our listeners. One of the most important lessons I learned from LEND was the value sharing my experience had when communicating with lawmakers. Being able to talk about the particulars of a bill is important, so is having handy fact sheets, statistics, and other supplemental material. However, the most compelling information I had to convey was the impact a piece of legislation would have on a constituent like me. Legislators no doubt go to congress with their own priorities, but they are supposed to represent us, and they very much want to be re-elected. Caught up in a storm of requests, obligations, and demands coming from all sides, a legislator may not be sure which way to go. My story could be their compass.

The legislation I chose to highlight during the Hill visits was the Autism CARES Act. The Autism CARES Act began life as the Combating Autism Act of 2006, was reauthorized under that name in 2011, reauthorized as Autism CARES in 2014, and now was scheduled to sunset in September 2019. A major piece of legislation, Autism CARES, is best described by its acronym CARES:

- COLLABORATION between the CDC, NIH, and other federal agencies through the establishment of the Interagency Autism Coordinating Committee.
- ACCOUNTABILITY to the public through reports to congress on the health and well-being of people throughout their lifespan.
- RESEARCH into autism prevalence, etiology, biomarkers, co-morbidities, and therapies.
- EDUCATION of health care professionals, people with disabilities, and members of their families through the sponsorship of Leadership Education in Neurodevelopmental and Related Disabilities (LEND) Programs.
- SUPPORT for families through the Autism Intervention Research Network on Physical Health (AIR-P), a national system of medical centers offering comprehensive care to children and adolescents with autism.

As I pointed out during the Hill visits, in addition to taking a comprehensive, multipronged approach to a complex condition impacting the individual, the family, and society, the Autism CARES

Act, through its sponsorship of LEND, also made me a better informed and more engaged citizen.

I also noted the progress I'd seen. Though the situation was far from perfect, I could attest to how much things had improved since my own autism diagnosis over a quarter-century earlier. Thanks in part to federal funding for research and data collection, we now know far more about autism and the best ways to provide treatment, services, and support.

When the Autism CARES Act was signed into law and reauthorized right before the September deadline, I took pride in the victory. I felt a sense of accomplishment in the part I played, small though it was, in the success of a major advocacy effort that involved an alliance of disability organizations from across the country. For me, it was an advancement. I'd been involved with promoting legislation in the state of Massachusetts. Now, I had moved up to the federal level.

But my greatest achievement was in finally finishing this book and telling my story. By completing what my mother and I had started, our joint writing project about my life with autism, I was carrying on her legacy. And though my mother wasn't there to write with me, her spirit was always guiding me. I can still hear her voice. I am always aware of her perspective, and I often find myself reacting to things with what feels like her response. My mother's words will always be with me, and filtered through my own experience and understanding, they will continue to assist me in making sense of the world.

Acknowledgments

I n his book, <u>Nobody's Normal</u>, medical anthropologist Richard Roy Grinker shares an insight he learned from the Jan/oansi, hunter-gatherers from remote villages in Namibia's Kalahari Desert. In telling the story of Geshe, a nine-year-old boy who cannot speak, Dr. Grinker describes how "when I asked the father if he is concerned about who will take care of Geshe after he and his wife pass away, he looked confused and then pointed to his neighbors. 'We won't all die at once,' he said" (4-5).

Even though I live in a more individualistic culture than the Jan/oansi, I still benefited from a similar sense of community after my mother passed away. The village rallied around me. Cathy Boyle started an e-mail chain connecting me with a Tribe of Autism Moms. Bob DiCesare, Leo Keenan, and David Malloy helped me move furniture and downsize. Bonnie Heligman sent me flowers, and Randy Lucus treated me to lunch. And that's just the tip of the iceberg. I got so much support from so many people that I could never do them all justice.

Then, there are the people who assisted me with this book. Liz Fancher read an early draft, Christopher McDougle guided me through several iterations, Pietro Miozzo offered many incisive comments, and Eve Megargel helped me rethink parts of the manuscript. I apologize to anyone whose name I neglected to mention. Just know that I appreciate whatever you did for me, and even if I don't happen to remember it at this moment, I will never truly forget it.

About The Author

Gyasi Burks-Abbott is a writer and public speaker who serves on the boards, committees, and commissions of several disability and autism organizations. A graduate of Macalester College in St. Paul, MN, with a BA in English and psychology, he is also a trained librarian with an M.S. in Library and Information Science from Simmons University in Boston. Currently, Gyasi is on the faculty of the LEND (Leadership Education in Neurodevelopmental and Related Disabilities) Program at Boston Children's Hospital and UMass Boston's Institute for Community Inclusion. He lives in Bedford, Massachusetts.

Printed in the USA
CPSIA information can be obtained
at www.ICGtesting.com
LVHW021054280424
778684LV00003B/624